Praise for
How to Become a Millionaire

'Investment is commonly thought to be a complicated game. But behind the jargon it is much more straight-forward than most believe. This book takes a no nonsense approach and will help any reader to a fuller understanding of the principles of effective and profitable money management.'

– Robert Cole, editor of the Tempus investment column
in *The Times*

'If anyone knows the secret of becoming a millionaire it is Jim Slater. He has done it himself more than once. His original approach combined with the measured thinking of Tom Stevenson, who is one of the country's most respected journalists, have produced a book that is both a page-turner and a work of reference.'

– Terry Bond, private investor, and a director of ProShare

'Jim Slater has a rare knack for explaining complex financial concepts in simple language that skilled and first-time investors alike can appreciate. If you believe that shares and property are the places to put your money in the coming years, you cannot fail to benefit from reading this book.'

– Jonathan Davis, investment columnist, *The Independent*, and chairman of Investor Publishing

'*How to Become a Millionaire* shows how to progress and become a more active private investor.'

– *Sunday Express*

'Slater outlines a formula for buying shares and cites mastery of the concept of compounding as the key to wealth. Investors of a wide range of ages are used as examples to show just how easy the plan is.'

– Moneywise

'Even by his critics he is acknowledged as a master investor with an innate sense of market timing. Tutors of his quality don't come along every day. Drink deep.'

– Shares magazine

HOW TO BECOME
A MILLIONAIRE

WARNING

Shares, unit trusts and investment trusts and the income from them can go down as well as up. When you seek advice, also ask about marketability. The shares, unit and investment trusts referred to in the text of this book are for illustrative purposes only and are not an invitation to deal in them. This book was completed in July 2000 and fully updated in June 2002. Since then market conditions have changed.

The systems for selecting shares described in the book are based on historical performance. There is no guarantee that these systems will work in the future, as market conditions may be very different.

Neither the publisher nor the authors accept any legal responsibility for the contents of the work, which is not a substitute for detailed professional advice. Readers should conduct their own investment activity through an appropriately authorised person.

HOW TO BECOME
A MILLIONAIRE

MAKE MONEY WHILE YOU SLEEP

JIM SLATER
TOM STEVENSON

J. S. Andrades

12 · 10 · 2002

TEXERE

New York • London

Copyright © 2000, 2002 J. D. Slater and Tom Stevenson

First Published in Great Britain in 2000 by TEXERE Publishing Limited

This edition published in 2002 by

TEXERE Publishing Limited
71–77 Leadenhall Street
London EC3A 3DE

Tel: +44 (0)20 7204 3644
Fax: +44 (0)20 7208 6701
www.etexere.co.uk

A subsidiary of

TEXERE LLC
55 East 52nd Street
New York, NY 10055

Tel: +1 (212) 317 5511
Fax: +1 (212) 317 5178
www.etexere.com

TEXERE books may be purchased for educational, business or sales
promotional use. For more information, please write to the Special Markets
Department at the TEXERE London address.

Project managed by Macfarlane Production Services, Markyate,
Hertfordshire, England (e-mail: macfarl@aol.com)

A CIP catalogue record for this book is available from the British Library

ISBN 1-58799-152-7

Typeset by MHL Typesetting Limited, Coventry, Warwickshire
Printed and bound in Great Britain by T J International Limited, Padstow,
Cornwall

This book is printed on acid-free paper responsibly manufactured from sus-
tainable forestry, in which at least two trees are planted for each one used
for paper production.

CONTENTS

PREFACE

A great deal has changed in the investment world since we wrote the first edition of this book. A huge speculative bubble in technology shares has been and gone, making and then losing many fortunes. The major economies of the world have flirted with recession and, thanks to a co-ordinated reduction in interest rates to levels not seen for 40 years, begun tentatively to grow once more. The housing market has defied the sceptics – and, some would say, gravity – as the low cost of borrowing has made bricks and mortar seem as safe as, well, houses.

Against this turbulent backdrop, we were initially nervous about revising *How To Become a Millionaire* – concerned that the central premise of the book, the wondrous combination of long-term investment in residential property and the stock market, would no longer stand up to scrutiny. It seemed possible, after two difficult years for the stock market, that updating the book would require a rethink of our blueprint for financial security.

It has been gratifying, therefore, to reach the conclusion that the central thrust of *How To Become a Millionaire* remains unchanged. No-one can forecast the future with any certainty, but it seems as likely today as it did two years ago that, in the long run, investing in property and shares is the surest way to a prosperous retirement. Combining these two investments in the way we suggest means you should benefit from the financial world's most exciting double whammy.

It is also even more true today than it was two years ago that anyone seriously interested in becoming a millionaire should avoid endowment policies like the plague. A combination of high charges and poor investment performance has made these among the worst savings vehicles available. Two years ago, 15 per cent of endowment policy holders were warned they would most likely not receive enough to pay off their mortgages. That proportion has now risen to 34 per cent, with a further 26 per cent being warned of a possible shortfall. If you are unlucky enough to be saddled with an endowment, Chapter 5 shows you how to assess whether or not to sell or surrender your policy and, if appropriate, how to get the most for it.

The only change worth highlighting here is one of emphasis. When we wrote the first edition of *How To Become a Millionaire* the stock market had enjoyed a remarkable 17 year bull market, possibly the greatest the world has ever seen. Against that backdrop, the most sensible approach for the non-specialist investor was to sit back and let the market weave its magic by investing in a tracker fund – a type of fund designed to do no more nor less than match the performance of the market as a whole. When the market had returned 18 per cent a year for 20 years there was little incentive to try and beat it.

It now seems likely that the returns from the stock market over the next few years will be somewhat less exciting than for most of the 1980s and 1990s. We, therefore, recommend even more than before the active investment approaches we describe in Chapters 9, 10 and 11. It may well be that, on balance, you would rather let someone else do your investing for you and you will stick to a tracker fund, but in coming to a decision you need to realise that the past two decades were an aberration – albeit a pretty exciting one for stock market investors.

We still believe that investing regularly in the stock market through a tracker fund will, in the long run, make you wealthy. But to be absolutely sure of becoming a millionaire, you will have to go the extra mile and learn how to be an active investor.

The beauty of the stock market is that some shares go up – sometimes spectacularly – even when the market as a whole is going sideways or backwards. If you follow the active methods in the later chapters you will stand a very good chance of investing in the winners and leaving the losers well alone.

There is less you can do about the other main element of your bid for financial freedom – investing well in residential property. Unlike with shares, a falling market is bad news for even the best houses in the most desirable locations. Here too, however, history is on your side. Anyone who bought a property at the height of the last boom in the late 1980s may have rued their bad timing for a few years in the early 1990s. But by now they are almost certainly sitting on a fantastic profit.

Investing in property and shares has another major advantage. Both of these assets work hard for you 24 hours a day, week in, week out, wherever you are and whatever you are doing. Buy well and you can sit back, relax and make money even while you sleep.

By buying this book, you have taken the first important step towards becoming a millionaire. Enjoy the ride.

ACKNOWLEDGEMENTS

Many people have helped us in the preparation of this book. Particular thanks are due to Anthony Bailey who has made an invaluable contribution to the chapters on buying and financing property, paying less tax and investing in tracker funds. Without his expert help it would have been a daunting task to write such a comprehensive blueprint for financial success.

We would both like to thank our wives for understanding that writing takes up a lot of time that might otherwise be spent with them and our children.

Thanks are once more due to Pam Hall, whose typing skills have once again borne the brunt of many drafts that each chapter goes through on its way to publication.

Last but not least, many thanks are due to Alan Purkiss for line-editing the final version. He made an invaluable contribution.

1

THE MIRACLE OF COMPOUNDING

'I am opposed to millionaires, but it would be dangerous to offer me the position.'

Mark Twain

The power of compounding is one of the world's best-kept secrets. An early understanding of its magic will transform your financial health.

Investing in property and shares can make you seriously rich. Not only in financial terms, but in the most important things money can buy – the time and the freedom to live life on your terms.

Even if you start with next to no savings, you will be able, with a little application, to secure financial freedom for yourself and for your family. It is hard to imagine a more sensible and attractive goal, yet most people will never achieve it.

The vast majority face a future of relative poverty because:

- they do not realise they can harness property and the stock market to accumulate substantial wealth
- they do not finance the purchase of their house or flat in the most effective manner
- they do not start saving early enough or shelter their savings from tax

- they underestimate the appalling toll inflation can take on the wealth they manage to create
- they do not know how to gain a competitive edge to become rich in real, inflation-adjusted terms.

IT REALLY COULD BE YOU

You have taken the first step towards financial freedom by buying this book. In it you will find a blueprint for financial security. We will show you how to become wealthy by buying your house or flat sensibly, financing it correctly and then systematically acquiring and managing a portfolio of unit trusts or shares. Building wealth in this way is not rocket science. You can be a successful investor whoever you are, wherever you live, whatever your age or sex.

How to Become a Millionaire is not a get-rich-quick scheme. If this is your fantasy, there are plenty of other publications to indulge it. Our focus is on the steady, relentless accumulation of real wealth through intelligent investment – it may be a more mundane goal, but it enjoys the merit of being both realistic and achievable. Unlike the lottery, in which the odds against winning the top prize are 14 million to one, the odds in property and stock market investment are stacked heavily in your favour. *It really could be you.*

THE FINANCIAL WORLD'S BEST-KEPT SECRET

Getting rich slowly and inexorably is not unduly complicated. It is achievable by simply harnessing a remarkable but well-kept secret – the extraordinary power of compounding. Tapping into this near miraculous force will set you on the road to great wealth and the sooner you start this profitable journey the greater your wealth will be.

Albert Einstein once called compounding the eighth wonder of the world. He was right. Compounding is a profoundly powerful force which, used with skill and patience, will provide you and your family with the warm glow and comfort of financial security for the rest of your lives. To gain the full benefit of this great gift you will need self-discipline and a willingness to learn the basics of investment. Time will do the rest.

What is compounding?

Compounding is a simple concept. If you increase a sum of money by the same percentage amount each year, the monetary value of each annual increase becomes progressively larger. If, for example, you start with £1,000 and grow your money by 10 per cent a year, the first year's increase is £100. The following year, however, the same 10 per cent rise is worth £110 because the starting capital is greater. Apply this growth rate repeatedly for 20 years, without withdrawing any capital, and the 10 per cent rise in the final year will be worth more than £600 – *six times the first year's increase.*

COMPOUNDING AND PROPERTY

Your family has probably already benefited from compounding. If, for example, you or your parents bought a house 25 years ago, you might have paid as little as £10,000 for it. Today, the same house is probably worth £200,000 or more.

This massive rise has been achieved because in almost every year since the house was bought its price increased by a small but significant percentage. Each year the percentage gain was applied to a larger starting figure until, slowly and relentlessly, the value of the house grew to a level that would have been scarcely imaginable at the outset.

You would not be all that surprised if the value of the £200,000 house were to rise over the next 12 months by £20,000, a far from exceptional 10 per cent. Compared with the initial purchase price, however, this increase alone is 200 per cent. Now look forward another 25 years. If the same £200,000 house rises in value by, say, 10 per cent a year over this period, it will be worth over £2 million. Even at 7 per cent a year, it will be worth £1 million and at 5 per cent £677,000.

The property market has the odds stacked in its favour because as people grow wealthier they are willing to spend a greater proportion of their income on housing. If someone earns £30,000 a year, they might be prepared to spend £10,000 a year on a mortgage, leaving £20,000 to live on. If their salary doubles to £60,000, however, they might be prepared to spend £25,000 on housing, assuming they are able to borrow this much, because this would still leave them with £35,000 to live on, much more than they previously enjoyed.

The doubling of their salary enables them to live in a house costing two and a half times as much while still enjoying a higher standard of living. This is one of the reasons why house prices grow faster than average earnings over time and why houses are likely to remain an excellent investment.

Another factor helping property prices in the UK is the old Mark Twain adage – they don't make land any more. The prices of houses or flats in prime positions, especially in capital cities like London, for example, can often rise to astronomic levels as there is a limited supply and there is always a great demand from overseas buyers as well as residents.

A further reason to use your house as part of your long-term investment planning is the fact that you can borrow a substantial percentage of the cost by taking out a mortgage. This can multiply many times the return on your original down payment. We therefore recommend that your first priority should be to buy your own home and we explain in detail in Chapter 3 the best way to go about this. In Chapter 4 we show you something equally important – how to finance your house purchase in the most flexible and tax-efficient way.

WEALTH YOU CAN ACTUALLY USE

The growth in the value of your house or flat is reassuring and, thanks to the leverage a mortgage provides, a vital element in anyone's bid to become a millionaire. It is, however, partly academic because *you have to live somewhere*. The money you make from your home tends to be realised only by your children after you die, unless you buy a smaller property in later life to release some of the capital tied up in your house. If you want to create the disposable wealth which will provide you with financial freedom while you can still enjoy it, you need an additional, more flexible investment than bricks and mortar.

Fortunately, the extraordinary compound growth the property market has experienced can also be obtained in the stock market. When the FTSE 100 index was introduced in 1984 to measure the performance of the UK's leading shares, it had a value of 1,000. After 18 years, the index is now over 5,000. A £10,000 investment in 1984 in a fund tracking the FTSE 100 would be worth about

£50,000 today. However, and this is where things begin to get interesting, if the next 18 years are as bountiful, the original £10,000 investment will have grown by 2020 to £250,000. In the last year alone, your gain would be over £20,000, twice your original investment.

You might be surprised to learn that the figures shown above are actually a *huge understatement* of the returns you can realistically expect to produce by investing directly in shares. The first reason the figures understate the potential is that the FTSE 100 index represents an average. Later we will show you how to produce *above-average* returns from your investments. Boosted by the power of compounding, this will make a massive difference to your ultimate wealth.

Secondly, the index ignores the dividend income from your shares. As you will see, reinvesting income rather than spending it is one of the most powerful means of enhancing your wealth. You might think it does not matter whether or not you reinvest the income from your shares, because it only represents 2 or 3 per cent of the value of your portfolio. However, the difference between achieving a return of 10 per cent a year from your shares and 13 per cent *over an extended* period is surprisingly large. For example, if you start with £10,000 and it grows by 10 per cent a year for 25 years you will end up with £108,000. If, by reinvesting your dividends, you achieve a 13 per cent return, your £10,000 will grow to £212,000. This is why it is so important to reinvest your dividends.

PROPERTY AND SHARES WORKING TOGETHER

The growth in UK property and share prices in recent years shows that both of these financial assets can rise in value materially over time. We have seen some of the reasons property has been such a good investment. Shares are attractive because they represent the most direct link with the growth of the economy. This has helped them to be the best performing financial asset over many decades. In the long run, boosted by the power of compounding, shares are by far the best place for your investments other than your own home.

The beauty of our blueprint for financial freedom is that it enables you to benefit very simply from a double whammy. We will show you how to use the stock market to finance your house purchase. You really can have the best of both worlds, benefiting from investing in two superb financial assets *at the same time.*

To see how this works in practice, imagine a 25-year-old man – we will call him Arthur – who buys a £100,000 flat with a 90 per cent mortgage. By agreement with his lender, he plans to repay the mortgage at the end of its term using his stock market investments. Instead of making small capital repayments every month he just pays interest on the loan and invests using a simple and relatively safe tax-free plan, which we will describe in detail in later chapters. Arthur starts saving £250 a month with a view to paying off his £90,000 mortgage in 20 years' time. Now jump forward 20 years to see how Arthur has fared. His investments have performed well, but not unusually so, averaging, say, 15 per cent a year total return over the period after all charges. By saving regularly, he has managed to generate a fund worth just over £300,000, more than three times the amount he needs to pay off his mortgage.

In the meantime, the value of his property has also soared, thanks to the relentless power of compounding. Let us assume that residential property has not quite kept up with the stock market over the 20 years but it has still achieved an average growth rate of 10 per cent a year. This means Arthur's £100,000 flat is now worth £673,000.

Adding together the value of Arthur's shares and that of his property, he is now, at the age of 45, worth almost £1 million. Even after paying off the £90,000 mortgage, Arthur is worth around £900,000. Without taking any undue risks, Arthur is set to become a millionaire well before his 50th birthday and he should have another 30 years or so of profitable investing ahead of him.

RELENTLESS GROWTH

Barclays Capital, the investment banking arm of the high street bank, conducts an excellent annual survey of financial assets with data stretching back to the beginning of the 20th century. It shows, for example, that £100 invested in the stock market in 1899, with all dividend income reinvested and ignoring any tax payments, would have been worth £1 million by the end of 2001. Over the same period, the same investment in government securities, or gilts, also with income reinvested, would have grown to just £15,600. Left in the bank or building society over the 100-year period, the £100 would have been worth only £14,300. Long-term, as the table below shows clearly, shares leave every other financial asset standing.

Value of £100 Invested at the End of 1899, Income Reinvested Gross

	Nominal	Real
Equities	£1,050,263	£19,671
Gilts	£15,556	£291
Cash	£14,349	£269

Source: Barclays Capital

What is interesting about these hugely different performances is that they are produced by the long-term compounding of a relatively small difference in average return each year. In the past 20 years, for example, shares *with dividends reinvested and after allowing for inflation* have produced a total real return of 10.9 per cent a year while gilts have achieved 8.2 per cent. This is only a small outperformance in any one year, but compounded, year after year, the benefit of the slightly higher return is a wonder to behold.

The first lesson of compounding, therefore, is that you must invest in the best-performing financial assets over time in order to achieve the highest long-term return. There is no guarantee that property and shares will continue to outperform all other asset classes but, if past performance is any guide, it looks to be a near certainty.

REINVESTING YOUR DIVIDENDS

A key element of building up your capital is the reinvestment of dividends. The Barclays Capital study shows that, had all dividends been spent as they were received, the £100 invested in 1899 would have grown to only £10,400 by 2001, compared with the £1 million achieved when all income was immediately reinvested. The reason for this is simple – dividend income makes up a significant proportion of the total return from shares and, as we have seen, even a small difference in each year's return, when compounded over a long period, can make a huge difference.

Even over shorter periods, the effect of reinvesting dividend income is dramatic. A £100 investment made in 1945 would have grown to £6,500 without reinvesting dividends. Ploughing the income back into the market would have produced £84,000.

This highlights the need for self-discipline in your investment. To reap the full benefits of compounding you need to save regularly in the early years and reinvest your dividend income. Fortunately, it is possible to set up an account with a stockbroker which will either reinvest your dividends automatically or at the very least leave them in your account as cash pending reinvestment. This will help you to resist temptation when dividend cheques drop through the letter-box.

TAXATION

The marked difference compounding can make to a relatively small improvement in annual return raises another important point – the need to shelter as much of your funds as possible from the ravages of taxation. For a higher rate taxpayer, failing to take advantage of the generous breaks on offer from the government can prove extremely costly in the long run. When compounding gets to work on your investments, the annual capital gains tax allowance should quickly be left behind so it is vital to shelter gains above this level.

We will show you how to use Individual Savings Accounts (ISAs) to create a substantial tax-free fund, compounding year after year free of capital gains and income taxes. Anyone who warns you that the extra charges you will incur with an ISA outweigh the tax advantages has not even begun to understand the power of compounding.

Someone investing the annual ISA allowance of £7,000 for 10 years, and achieving a demanding but not unrealistic annual return of 15 per cent, would have a tax-sheltered sum of more than £170,000 by the end of the period. For a man and wife, the amount could be double this. The annual charge for ISAs is often capped at a fairly low level, so for anyone saving their full allowance it quickly pales into insignificance.

START EARLY

The arithmetic of investment is very simple. The final value of your investment fund is the product of four factors:

1. When you start.
2. How much money you contribute.
3. The rate of return you achieve each year.
4. The length of time you are able to let compounding weave its magic spell.

We have already seen that shares are the best-performing asset class over the long run and doing no more than tracking the market should set you well on the way to becoming a millionaire. In later chapters we will also show you how to select above-average shares to allow you to reach your goal even more quickly. Selecting shares well is obviously essential, but the most important weapon in your investment armoury is available to all, absolutely free – it is quite simply time. The sooner you understand the impact of time on the power of compounding, the richer you will become. It really is as easy as that.

Consider the story of 25-year-old twin sisters – we will call them Prudence and Extravaganza. Prudence has just finished reading *How to Become a Millionaire* and has decided to save £1,000 a year, starting in 2002, which she invests in the stock market. Let us say that she benefits from a consistent return of 15 per cent a year.

After 10 years, Extravaganza, who has been living it up in style, sees how well her sister is doing and starts to invest the same amount, £1,000 a year. She also achieves a return of 15 per cent a year. Just as Extravaganza starts saving and investing, Prudence stops. She never puts another penny into her investment fund, although like her sister she continues to achieve a 15 per cent return each year.

Now jump forward to the year 2036, when the twins turn 60. Prudence, you remember, stopped investing in 2012, having contributed £10,000 to her fund. Extravaganza contributed £25,000 in the 25 years between 2012 and 2036. Who has the bigger retirement fund, Prudence or Extravaganza?

The table opposite shows the value of the sisters' savings each year between 2002 and 2036. Because of the extraordinary power of compounding, Prudence's nest-egg is worth £670,000 when she retires. Extravaganza's is worth less than a third of that, £213,000, even though she paid in two and a half times more than her sister. *Prudence's fund is worth so much more simply because she started earlier. No matter how long Extravaganza continues to pay into her fund, she will never catch up with her sister.*

IT IS NEVER TOO LATE

The story of Prudence and Extravaganza shows that you need to start saving now if you are to tap the full potential of the power of compounding. Once you have built up a meaningful fund, small amounts of regular saving will

Starting Early

End of Year	Prudence	Extravaganza	End of Year	Prudence	Extravaganza
2002	1,000	0	2020	71,427	16,786
2003	2,150	0	2021	82,141	20,304
2004	3,473	0	2022	94,462	24,350
2005	4,993	0	2023	108,631	29,002
2006	6,742	0	2024	124,926	34,352
2007	8,754	0	2025	143,665	40,505
2008	11,067	0	2026	165,215	47,581
2009	13,727	0	2027	189,997	55,718
2010	16,786	0	2028	218,497	65,076
2011	20,304	0	2029	251,271	75,837
2012	23,350	1,000	2030	288,962	88,213
2013	26,852	2,150	2031	332,306	102,445
2014	30,880	3,473	2032	382,152	118,811
2015	35,512	4,993	2033	439,475	137,633
2016	40,839	6,742	2034	505,396	159,278
2017	46,964	8,754	2035	581,205	184,170
2018	54,009	11,067	2036	668,386	212,795
2019	62,110	13,727			

make little difference to your eventual wealth. *The key to investment is building capital in the early years.* You cannot afford to wait; the earlier you start, the richer you will be.

However, even if you understand the power of compounding later than Prudence, it really is never too late to start investing. Because compounding is such a powerful force, you can make a significant difference to your financial well-being by investing intelligently for as little as five or ten years.

Consider a 60-year-old man who has just reached the retirement age he elected when he started his personal pension. Under current legislation he is allowed to withdraw a quarter of his total pension fund, tax-free, while using the other three quarters to purchase an annuity.

His permitted withdrawal might be £50,000 or more. A meaningful sum like this, invested using one of the systematic methods we will explain later in the book and producing an average annual return of 15 per cent, might be worth as much as £100,000 when the man is 65 or over £200,000 by the time he turns 70. With life expectancy growing ever greater, retirement could mark the beginning of a long, lucrative and very enjoyable second career as an investor.

SAVE HARD

A vital element in the compounding equation – how much you can contribute – is a personal matter. Needless to say, it makes sense to save and invest as much as you reasonably can. Life is always a trade-off between current and future consumption, but if you resist the temptation to spend today you will reap the benefit many times over tomorrow.

It is amazing how simple it is to save the relatively modest amounts you need to become a millionaire. At more than £4 a packet, it is easy for a smoker to get through £1,000 a year on cigarettes, for example. If you do not smoke you probably spend a similar amount on some other indulgence. As Prudence showed, investing even this small amount over a long period could transform your financial health.

The best way to understand why this matters so much is to think about the consequences of not saving now. Let us assume you are 65 and have never saved a penny throughout your working life. The state pension is barely enough to survive on so you might decide to put your gardening skills to work to supplement your income. Say you work about 15 hours a week and earn £10 an hour. This might not be what you had in mind for your retirement but you may have little choice. Your weekly income would be £150 or around £7,500 a year.

Now remember 20 years ago when, aged 45, you received a modest inheritance from a relative of £3,000 and used it to replace your car with a newer model. Why not? It was only £3,000 and that wasn't going to make much difference to your life. However, if you had invested that £3,000 in the stock market and for the next 20 years achieved the 15 per cent a year overall return we believe is a reasonable target for most investors, it would now be worth £49,000, which at 15 per cent would produce an annual overall income of £7,400 a year. In other words, you would be able to match your current hard-earned income for the rest of your life, with almost no effort, entirely due to a relatively small sacrifice all those years ago.

Of course, it is possible that you will fail to achieve a 15 per cent return. When we first wrote this book in 2000, the stock market had returned 18 per cent a year for 20 years, but it is now widely believed that the 1980s and 1990s were exceptional years for the stock market. Even 15 per cent a year may be too demanding a target over an extended period, but we firmly believe that the strategies for consistently beating the market that we will show you make it an achievable one.

No-one is suggesting you should stop enjoying life to the full now because of what might happen many years hence. We all run the risk of falling under a bus tomorrow. But it is important to understand that the power of compounding imbues our financial decisions today with enormous future consequences.

THE RULE OF 72

A useful rule of thumb for measuring the power of compounding is the Rule of 72. Its purpose is to give an idea of the number of years it takes to double the size of an investment fund at a given rate of annual return.

The rule is easy to use. Simply divide the expected growth rate into 72. The resultant number shows approximately how many years it will take to double an investment. For example, at 12 per cent a year, it will take six years to turn £1,000 into £2,000. If you only achieve 6 per cent a year it will take 12 years to double your money.

On the basis of our target return of 15 per cent, it should, therefore, be possible to double your money every five years or so (72 divided by 15 equals around 5). Thanks to the power of compounding, this means that after 10 years, your investment should have grown four-fold. After 15 years it will have grown by a factor of eight, after 20 years by 16 times and after 25 years by 32 times. Notice how quickly the return on your initial investment accelerates in the later years.

To achieve an average growth rate of 15 per cent a year for 25 years would be impressive because it is inevitable that you will have some poor years. Also, the larger your fund grows, the more difficult it is to produce above-average results. However, this is not an unreasonable target for an active investor.

If you have savings of £32,000, it is within your power to generate a fund worth £1 million over the next 25 years or so, even if you save nothing more from now on. If you do not have this much to start with, or if you achieve a lower rate of return, you will need to save harder in the early years to give yourself a reasonable chance of reaching your £1 million target.

Even if, like most people, you are starting from scratch, and are unable to save a great deal, you will be able to achieve an impressive result. Emulating the performance of Prudence, who started with nothing and saved just £1,000 a year for the first 10 years only, would give you £165,000 after 25 years. *Add this to the growth over this period in the value of a flat or house and you can see that material wealth is within the reach of most people.*

FEELING CONFIDENT?

We hope this chapter has filled you with enthusiasm for the benefits you and your family can gain by investing in property and the stock market. Compounding is a wonderful force and gaining an early understanding of its power will change your life. Hopefully, your enthusiasm will sustain you through the next chapter, which is, deliberately, a more sobering read. Not that it will put you off the idea of property and stock market investment – quite the reverse, it should make you realise that harnessing the great power of compounding is not a luxury but a necessity.

In a perfect world, our shares and the value of our house or flat would rise steadily while the cost of everything we bought would stay the same. Unfortunately, life does not work this way. Investing in property and the stock market can help you become a millionaire but, unless the world changes completely, *you are going to need to.*

SUMMARY

1. The power of compounding is the financial world's best-kept secret. Used with skill and patience, it will

provide you and your family with the warm glow of financial security for the rest of your lives.

2. The property market has benefited enormously from the power of compounding and is likely to continue to do so. Make sure you own your own house or flat and use the stock market to finance its purchase in a flexible, tax-efficient way. With this double whammy, you can invest in two superb financial assets for the price of one.

3. Even if you only perform as well as the historical averages, you can become seriously rich by investing in the stock market. Tracking the averages can be achieved simply, with no specialist knowledge, with a wide range of pooled investments such as unit trusts.

4. Compounding even a small outperformance over the years will massively enhance your ultimate wealth. We will show you how to outperform the averages.

5. It is never too late to benefit from compounding but you should start investing as early as you can. The sooner you harness its power, the richer you will become.

6. Maximise your returns by reinvesting the dividends from your shares.

7. Save regularly and hard in the early years and shelter as much of your money as you can from tax.

8. The Rule of 72 shows you how quickly you can double your money at any rate of return. Simply divide 72 by the return to calculate the approximate number of years it will take to double your fund.

9. Always remember that, in the long run, the odds in property and stock market investment are stacked heavily in your favour. It really could be you.

2

INFLATION – THE SLEEPING DRAGON

'A billion here, a billion there and pretty soon you're talking about real money.'

Everett Dirksen

Inflation is not dead. It exacts an enormous toll on the purchasing power of your money. Buying property and shares is one of the few ways to protect yourself against it.

The previous chapter deliberately painted a rosy picture of the power of compounding and you are now probably looking forward to la dolce vita. *Your future life looks sweet in your £1 million house, watching your capital gains mount up as you push another million around the market. Unfortunately, this is only half the story, because compounding is a two-edged sword.*

It is a sad fact that the same force which will relentlessly increase the value of your investments is also working on the cost of living. Even a modest inflation rate, when compounded year after year, can drastically reduce the purchasing power of your savings and the real value of your house or flat. Unfortunately, you are going to need to run fast simply to stand still.

THE RAVAGES OF INFLATION

We have shown how you can use the stock market to create sums of money which are mind-boggling when looked at in today's terms. The bad news is that in 20 or 30 years' time a million or so is likely to have become run of the mill. If you are not a millionaire in 20 years time then there is a good chance that you will be relatively poor.

Back in the early 1960s, £1,000 a year would have been a good salary for a secretary in central London. Today the same job would probably pay £20,000 and £1,000 would not be enough to buy a decent holiday. Jump forward 40 years and imagine a world in which secretaries are taking home £400,000 a year (20 times £20,000, assuming inflation continues at the same rate). Suddenly a million pounds sounds rather paltry.

There is a sobering City joke about a man who went to sleep one night with £10,000 invested in shares. Like Rip Van Winkle, he stayed asleep for a hundred years and, on waking, called his broker to see how his portfolio was doing.

The broker was long dead, of course, but his grandson, who had taken over the business, informed the man that his portfolio was now worth £10 million. Overjoyed, he rushed out into the street to buy a newspaper to read about the great events that had caused this massive rise in the value of his investments. When he was asked for £250 for the news-paper, he was suddenly, and understandably, less jubilant.

TAMING THE MONSTER

Our Rip Van Winkle learned with a jolt that assets do not appreciate in value in isolation. Some assets tend to rise faster than others over time, *but the only sensible way to look at increases in value is in real, inflation-adjusted terms.* When the cost of living is rising fast, our financial assets need to rise even faster if they are to make us richer in a meaningful way.

A couple of years ago, an article in *The Daily Telegraph* showed the impact inflation has had over the previous 40 years on a typical shopping basket of consumer goods. In 1959, you would have paid the equivalent of 64p for a pound of butter, a pint of milk, a pint of beer, 20 cigarettes, a pound of apples and a loaf of bread. By 1999, the cost of the same items had soared to £8.44, a 13-fold increase.

During this 40-year period, inflation reached historically high levels, peaking at around 25 per cent in 1975. However, it would be wrong to think that the savage reduction in buying power over this period was the result of consistently high rises in the cost of living. As you can see from the cost of living table overleaf, before 1970 inflation reached 5 per cent only once, in 1968, and since 1983 it has been above this level relatively briefly. However, even at comparatively low levels, inflation can drastically reduce your purchasing power when its insidious effects are repeated year after year.

The Barclays cost of living data show that, even in the low-inflation 1960s, prices rose by 59 per cent between 1961 and 1971. More recently, the cost of living has increased by 28 per cent between 1991 and 2001. Certainly, the 1970s were appallingly inflationary years, and prices rose in that decade more than three times. However, it is the relentless single-digit rises during most of the rest of the 40-year period which has compounded into a 13-fold reduction in purchasing power in the past 40 years.

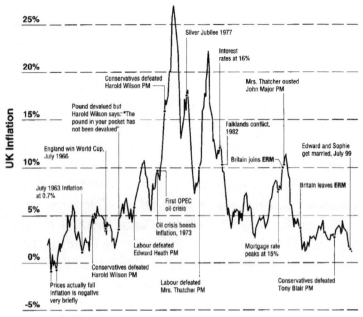

1959 Prices

Pound of butter	22p
Pint of milk	3p
Pint of beer	9p
20 cigarettes	20p
Pound of apples	5p
Loaf of bread	5p
TOTAL	**64p**

1999 Prices

Pound of butter	£1.51
Pint of milk	34p
Pint of beer	£1.94
20 cigarettes	£3.66
Pound of apples	48p
Loaf of bread	51p
TOTAL	**£8.44**

Source: *The Daily Telegraph*

The Rising Cost of Living

Year	Index	% change	Year	Index	% change
1962	416.5	2.6	1982	2,541.6	5.4
1963	424.2	1.9	1983	2,676.7	5.3
1964	444.6	4.8	1984	2,799.3	4.6
1965	464.5	4.5	1985	2,958.5	5.7
1966	481.6	3.7	1986	3,068.6	3.7
1967	493.4	2.5	1987	3,182.0	3.7
1968	522.7	5.9	1988	3,397.6	6.8
1969	547.1	4.7	1989	3,659.5	7.7
1970	590.3	7.9	1990	4,001.4	9.3
1971	643.6	9.0	1991	4,180.0	4.5
1972	692.9	7.7	1992	4,287.8	2.6
1973	766.2	10.6	1993	4,369.3	1.9
1974	912.8	19.1	1994	4,495.6	2.9
1975	1,140.0	24.9	1995	4,640.3	3.2
1976	1,311.8	15.1	1996	4,754.2	2.5
1977	1,471.1	12.1	1997	4,926.6	3.6
1978	1,594.4	8.4	1998	5,062.1	2.8
1979	1,869.3	17.2	1999	5,151.4	1.8
1980	2,151.9	15.1	2000	5,302.3	2.9
1981	2,411.2	12.0	2001	5,339.2	0.7

Index: 1899 = 100
Source: Barclays Capital

THE DEATH OF INFLATION?

Inflation is not the untamed beast that it has been in recent years, and with control over interest rates now out of the hands of the politicians it is arguably more likely that inflation will be kept in check in the future.

As we write, inflation is running at about 2 per cent a year, returning to levels we have not enjoyed since the

1960s. There are plausible arguments why technological advances and globalisation should have increased productivity and so reduced inflation. However, the price of oil has been extremely volatile in recent years and it would be a brave person who bet that the dragon of inflation had been killed off for good.

It would also be a most imprudent assumption to make when planning your financial future. We recommend that you assume inflation will continue to some degree so that instead of being disappointed you might be pleasantly surprised. If you do not factor in an increase in the cost of living, you are likely to be undone by your complacency.

WHAT WILL YOUR MILLION BUY?

The word 'millionaire' has an attractive ring to it and it is still true that the possession of a million pounds today makes you relatively rich. However, pause a moment to consider what has happened to the purchasing power of a million pounds. It has shrunk during the past 40 inflation-prone years to just £77,000 today.

Although inflation is very subdued currently, we think it would be prudent to assume that over the next 25 years the cost of living could rise by an average of 5 per cent a year. This level of erosion would reduce the buying power of a future million to about £300,000 in today's money. Now this is still a tidy sum, but if it was your net worth today you would not feel rich.

For a 65-year-old, for example, £300,000 would buy an annuity of about £22,000 a year *with no protection against future inflation*. Ten years later, with 5 per cent annual inflation, the buying power of this annuity would be reduced to about £15,000 in today's terms.

We hope it is becoming obvious that an apparently large sum today is likely to be much less attractive by the time you have accumulated it. *You, therefore, need to set your sights high.* At a 5 per cent rate of inflation, for example, you would need to accumulate over £3 million in 25 years' time to enjoy the same purchasing power as a millionaire today.

RUN FAST TO STAND STILL

Hopefully, inflation will not exact the same terrible toll on your savings in the future as it has in the past, and your final target figure will still have significant buying power in today's terms. *But you should be realising by now that you have to run fast simply to stand still even in a mildly inflationary environment.*

The most important first step in defeating inflation is to buy your own home. Residential property is an excellent hedge against rising prices. Then you should put your faith in the stock market and try to ensure you at least keep pace with the main market indices.

Matching the averages by buying tracker funds should help to make you a millionaire *in today's money as well as tomorrow's.* But if you want to be certain of achieving significant real wealth, you will need to outperform the averages. In later chapters we will show you how to do this, so you stand a very good chance of becoming truly wealthy.

SUMMARY

1. Inflation has exacted an enormous toll on the purchasing power of money in recent decades. Do not assume that the dragon of inflation has been slain.

2. If your aim is to be wealthy in real, inflation-adjusted terms, you should be able to achieve this by buying your own property and investing regularly in tracker funds.

3. If you want to be more certain of achieving significant real wealth, you need to gain a competitive edge over the market and other investors and beat the averages.

3

BUY YOUR OWN HOME

'Increased means and increased leisure are the two
civilizers of man.'

Benjamin Disraeli

Residential property was one of the best investments in the 20th century and it is likely to repeat the performance over the next 100 years. There are very strong financial arguments for investing in your own home, but in today's heady markets it is important to ensure that you look for property in as prime a position as possible and that you negotiate toughly using a checklist of key points.

From an investment point of view, owning a house or flat is preferable to renting and a key element of your bid for financial freedom. As with any other investment, it is helpful to first study past performance, so have a look at the graph overleaf showing what has happened to house prices and the cost of living since 1960.

As you can see, it was only in the 1970s that property took off in earnest. Inflation was also rocketing then and this is reflected in the steep rise in retail prices. In spite of a damaging slump in the early 1990s, property has kept well ahead of consumer inflation, especially in the last few years, and this trend is likely to continue.

A typical London house might have risen in price from £20,000 in the late 1970s to more than £400,000 today. Over 25 years, £20,000 to £400,000 compares very

Source: Nationwide, ONS

favourably indeed with other investments. In fact, the percentage gain would have been even better for most people as they would have arranged a mortgage to finance at least 60 per cent, and probably as much as 90 per cent, of the original cost. If they had borrowed 90 per cent, their net outlay would have been only £2,000 with a resultant capital profit of £380,000 after paying back the mortgage.

In addition, for much of the period, the interest on the £18,000 mortgage could have been charged against income for taxation purposes – tax relief on a mortgage for a property you buy to live in yourself was not finally abolished until April 2000. In contrast, rent would have had to be paid out of net income. As if this were not enough, the capital gain of £380,000 would have been free of tax. No wonder so many British people have been enriched by home ownership during the last few decades.

LOOKING AHEAD

More relevant to anyone starting out now is whether or not property will continue to be such a rewarding investment in the years ahead. No one can foretell the future, but we believe there are good reasons for being positive. Inflation could return at any time and, even if the rate of inflation remains relatively low, an investment in bricks and mortar is likely to retain its value in real terms.

As we have seen, the effects of inflation are insidious for savers, but the value of houses and flats in Britain has more than kept pace with rising consumer prices. If the value of a £100,000 home bought by a man and wife aged 30 rises by 5 per cent a year, by the time the couple reach 75 the house or flat will be worth around £900,000. Of course, there is no guarantee that price rises will average as much as 5 per cent but experience tells us that this is a real possibility.

At the start of 2002, the outlook for house prices is uncertain. With interest rates at their lowest level for around 40 years, the cost of servicing a mortgage is relatively low. This has fuelled a boom in house prices, which over the past year have risen by around 16 per cent on average.

Over time, house prices have tended to rise broadly in line with average earnings, with short periods of sometimes marked outperformance. The chart on the previous page shows clearly how prices soared above the long-term trend during the boom of the late 1980s and then came back to the long-run average as prices fell in the early 1990s while earnings continued to rise.

The chart shows that the recent surge in house prices has once again left earnings well behind and this is undoubtedly a cause for concern in the short term. When the linkage between house prices and earnings is broken in this way, first time buyers find it impossible to get a foot on the housing ladder and the lack of buyers at the bottom of the housing chain eventually causes the boom to fizzle out.

An added concern this time round is the rapid increase in the number of people taking out so-called buy-to-let mortgages. They are buying houses not to live in but as speculative investments and it is likely that if house prices start to fall they will try to liquidate their investments, putting further downward pressure on prices.

Most industry professionals in early 2002 believe, however, that the rate of growth in house prices will simply slow and we will avoid a crash like the one ten years ago which left so many buyers with outstanding mortgages greater than the value of their houses – negative equity as it was called.

History suggests that the forecasts of the professionals are about as reliable as the predictions of Gypsy Rose Lee on Brighton pier. And perhaps the best time to be sceptical is when they are all singing confidently from the same hymn sheet. You would feel aggrieved if you paid top whack at the peak of the market, only to see the value of your new home fall substantially.

A fall in prices may not be disastrous if you expect to live in your property for many years and history, insofar as it can be a guide, shows that the long-term trend of property prices is strongly upwards. But that will be little consolation if you want to move in the short term and find, after a couple of years, that the only way to sell your property is by accepting a substantial loss.

Do not worry unduly about these caveats. There is little doubt that owning your own house is a wonderful long-term investment. In today's heady markets, however, it is important to buy well, to check the position of the property very carefully, to use a detailed checklist of key points that need answering and to negotiate the price toughly.

FREEHOLD OR LEASEHOLD?

In England and Wales, buying a house freehold means you own outright the building and the land on which it stands. With a leasehold, you pay a lump sum for the right to occupy the house for an agreed period of years, subject to paying a ground rent, which can range from £20 or so a year to a few hundred pounds. At the end of that time, the land and buildings revert to the landlord.

In England and Wales, flats are invariably leasehold. As long as the freeholder is reasonable, there is no need to worry about this provided the lease is long. Over 80 years is regarded by valuers almost as a freehold and you will have no difficulty in selling the flat on when the time comes to move. If the lease is less than, say, 20 years, you should begin to regard it as a wasting asset and expect the value in real terms to decline a little each year. Obtaining a loan will also be more difficult. To be on the safe side, you should try to make sure that the lease of any flat you buy has well over 50 years to run, and preferably over 80.

In 1993, the Leasehold Reform, Housing and Urban Development Act was passed by Parliament, giving English and Welsh leaseholders, with leases with an original term of over 21 years, the right (subject to a large number of caveats) to extend those leases or purchase the freehold. In the case of a block of flats, this might be arranged on a collective basis by all of the tenants.

In Scotland, leasehold flats and houses are few and far between. Some properties have a charge called a feu duty attached, but these now have to be bought out when houses and flats are sold, so they are gradually disappearing.

LOCATION, LOCATION, LOCATION

The most important criterion when buying a property is position. The word 'position' in this context embraces the whole ambience of a property. In the country, for example, search for a house on high ground, surrounded by its own land, with panoramic views. You are looking for peace and quiet and control over your immediate environment. Although this is harder to achieve, exactly the same principle applies to buying flats and smaller houses in towns and cities.

The importance of location is thrown most starkly into relief when the property market turns down after a few years of strong growth. While prices are rising quickly, buyers can be unable to afford houses or flats in the best areas and they push further afield until they find a property in their price range.

Unfortunately, this pressure can lead to silly prices being paid for quite ordinary houses in relatively undesirable areas. In the late 1980s, for example, buyers priced out of newly-fashionable Clapham and Battersea in South London moved further out to less popular areas like Balham and Brixton. When prices fell back in the recession of the early 1990s, the better areas escaped relatively unscathed while buyers in the cheaper areas had their fingers badly burned.

The best way to make money in the property market is to catch, at a relatively early stage, an area which is being 'gentrified'. Tell-tale signs include a rash of new openings of wine bars, delicatessens and 'upmarket' shops. Watch out for skips, too – a sure sign that relatively wealthy buyers are moving in and stripping out the 'bad taste' of their predecessors.

The second easy way to make good profits from

residential property is to buy a type of property which has been out of favour and is becoming more fashionable. For example, 40 years ago no-one wanted to live in Victorian terraced houses, because they were not 'modern'. Now they are the height of sophistication.

An even more extreme example is provided by the amazing growth in the value of old Georgian rectories. In the 1950s and 1960s, the Church sold many of these houses for a relative pittance because no-one wanted to live in big, draughty old piles. Today, you need to be extremely wealthy to even consider buying one of these beautiful properties.

A BUYER'S CHECKLIST

Buying your own home is the largest purchase most people ever make so it is vital to be very thorough. Here is a checklist of the points to consider:

1. Attractive views from the windows and garden, if any, are an obvious advantage.
2. South and west-facing is usually preferable, as the living rooms enjoy more hours in the sun.
3. Winter light is very different from summer light. This is particularly important for houses or flats overlooked by large buildings, or country houses with hills nearby. A friend quizzed the owner of a house in a valley on whether his sitting room, basking in the July sun, ever enjoyed the winter light. He admitted that it did not and also mentioned that no other prospective purchaser had asked that question.
4. An attractive garden is valuable, especially in a block of flats where only yours has access to and respon-

sibility for the garden. Similarly, a balcony to catch the sun is desirable.

5. In big cities, parking is increasingly difficult, so a garage or easy parking for residents is an advantage.

6. A top flat can be the most attractive in a block, provided there is a lift. Otherwise, too many steps are only for the young and athletic, restricting the number of potential buyers when you come to sell.

7. In cities, avoid basement flats (usually described by estate agents as lower ground floor). They are bad for security, dark and often suffer from damp.

8. Check whether or not the house or flat is on a flight path or likely to be on one. Similarly, your survey should check if any roads are likely to be diverted your way or new ones built nearby. A tube line running underneath your house or flat can also be a disadvantage.

9. *Always* inspect the property at night as well as during the day. Many neighbours will be home from work then and you can assess the noise level better. The road may be busier with night lorries or, if the houses have no garages, you may find that there are too many parked cars in the road.

10. Bad neighbours, who make a lot of noise and are inconsiderate, are to be avoided like the plague. Not only will they annoy you, but they will also make it far more difficult for you to sell advantageously when the time comes. Checking up on future neighbours can be done in two ways. First, have a good look at their garden and the state of repair of their house or flat. Then knock on their door and tell them that you are thinking of buying the house or flat nearby, would like to meet them and wonder if they have any advice to offer. If they are going to be the right neighbours, they will welcome your initiative. If not, far better to find out before signing the contract.

11. It is usually bad news to be near a pub, restaurant, massage parlour or youth hostel or too near a railway station. All are prone to extra activity with the risk of rowdiness, often late at night.

12. Access to good schools, shops, a railway station and buses are excellent selling points.

13. Having space to expand is a big advantage. Bear in mind that there are additional restrictions for listed buildings and for those in a conservation area. In a few years' time, the possibility of adding a room to your house might make all the difference to your family.

14. Storage space is important, so welcome walk-in cupboards and built-in wardrobes.

15. Gas central heating and cooking facilities are usually to be preferred. They are cheaper, more efficient and easier to control.

16. With houses in particular, watch out for large trees that might be too near the property. The first danger is from roots and the second from storm damage.

17. Houses near to rivers are to be avoided if the lie of the land makes flooding a possibility. In recent years, this has become an increasing issue as changing weather patterns have made floods an almost annual event. Despite this, access to trout or coarse fishing at a safe distance can be a very useful selling point.

18. The porter in a block of flats can be a very helpful source of information about other tenants and possible problems. With a country house, a visit to the village pub can be very informative.

A COMMON SENSE SURVEY

If you decide to buy a house or flat, you will need to arrange for a professional survey. However, to save money, first do a common sense survey on your own to eliminate any prospect that has obvious faults.

For a start, visit the property at least twice. You will often find that it is not as good as you first thought, especially if you make the second visit at night. It is important to keep your main objective firmly in mind. Try not to be distracted by side-issues like the seductive smell of coffee being ground or bread baking or, for example, by minor architectural features like attractive cornices or special brass door fittings. Concentrate instead upon how you will use the property you buy. Consider the number of floors and the practicalities of the layout. Check the essentials and make sure that the rooms are the right size, the property is in good condition and will meet your family's requirements. Here is a further checklist of some of the more mundane points to concentrate on during your common sense survey:

1. Make sure that all the bathrooms, toilets and kitchens have proper ventilation.
2. Look, not only at eye level, for damp patches, stains, peeling wallpaper, flaking plaster and mould.
3. Check beams, doors and other woodwork for woodworm holes. They are usually easy to see.
4. Check outside walls for cracks and make sure the roof appears to be level and is not sagging. Also, keep an eye open for holes in the guttering and slipped slates.
5. A musty smell could be caused by dry rot, which can be very expensive and messy to deal with.
6. Remember that furniture and pictures that have been in place for some time may have caused discoloration, making redecoration necessary. If the current owner is a heavy smoker, there will usually be yellow stains.
7. Remember that furniture often hides carpet stains and

both large and small pieces of furniture can sometimes dramatically alter your perception of a room. Much of the charm and atmosphere of a property may be due to the contents and the way they are arranged. Once they are taken away, substantial redecoration may be required and much of the charm lost.

8. Imagine your own furniture positioned throughout the flat or house. In particular, check the kitchen area to make sure there is enough room for your washing machine, dishwasher, fridge, freezer, microwave and the like.

9. Check the measurements of each room. Not to the inch, but make sure that they are broadly in line with the sales particulars.

10. Rotten window frames are quite common and easy to see from the outside. Curtains can hide the condition of inside windows, so pull them back to have a good look and make sure that they work properly.

11. Lead pipes and tanks are undesirable.

12. Ask about insulation, especially in the roof. This can save a great deal of money in heating bills.

13. Check the main fuse board and sockets and make sure that they appear to be modern. Sockets should be 13 amp, preferably with more than one in each room. Lead-covered cables and old cord wiring are bad news.

14. Cracks, leaning doors and frames and sloping floors are usually evidence of subsidence.

15. In a block of flats, check the outgoings and management charges in detail. The management has the right to charge only reasonable fees for running the building. Check if there is a sinking fund to cover common repairs and renovations if not you might suddenly be asked to contribute a large sum. Also, ask about common repair bills. If you are buying a top flat, you

should make sure that you do not have sole or disproportionate responsibility for roof repairs. If the flat is on the ground floor, check whether any contribution has to be made to maintenance of the lift.

NEGOTIATING THE PRICE

Once you have finished your common sense survey, you have to decide whether or not to proceed with a full survey. To have gone this far, you obviously like many features of the property. However, the unsatisfactory points that you discovered during your common sense survey may outweigh the plus points. If you still feel on balance that you want the property, you should use the list of criticisms to negotiate a reduced price.

Your ability to negotiate will depend on market conditions. In the housing boom of the late 1990s and early years of the new century, in certain parts of the country, some sellers found so much interest from buyers that they ended up achieving more than their asking price. However, in quieter markets and all house price booms eventually fizzle out – almost everyone is prepared to negotiate.

Take, for example, a flat with an asking price of £82,500. When you are told the suggested price, you should shake your head sorrowfully, inform the agent it is too high and point out that a lot of work needs doing. List the problems one by one and end up offering, say, £75,000. The agent may then suggest £80,000 and you might eventually settle at £77,500 after a little more haggling.

Now comes the most important single point. Your offer should always be made *subject to contract and survey*, and these important words should always appear on any letters originating from you. They will ensure that you cannot be held to the deal if your surveyor finds a hidden problem. If the owner accepts your offer, you may be asked to make a small deposit to show good faith. There is no harm in this provided the deposit is made with the estate agent or the owner's solicitor. Make sure, too, that the receipt clearly indicates that the deposit is refundable if, for any reason, you decide not to proceed. (The law is different in Scotland – you should get legal advice if you are unsure about the practice there.)

At this point, you will see that you have not yet had to use and pay for any professional services. You have kept costs to an absolute minimum by doing the common sense survey yourself and conducting the negotiation. You may have to look closely at a large number of houses or flats before you make a final choice, so do not waste money on professional fees on prospects that fail to match your requirements.

APPOINTING A SOLICITOR

If you do not have a solicitor of your own, ask close friends or able business associates to recommend theirs. There is no better introduction than a strong recommendation from someone you know well and respect. Ask the solicitor to give you a written estimate of likely charges – if they seem exorbitant, you can cross-check with other solicitors. The written estimate will also help to pin down the charges when your solicitor presents his final bill.

Your solicitor will conduct a search on likely developments in the area, such as new roads and housing estates. He will also arrange for land registration, payment of stamp duty of 1 per cent on the whole of the purchase price, if over £60,000, (3 per cent if over £250,000 and 4 per cent if over £500,000), exchange of final contracts and completion, which is usually a month afterwards. You do not have to be present during completion. Your solicitor can pass over your cheque, exchange documents and obtain the keys for you to move in.

Completion can, in fact, take place on the same day as you exchange contracts. You do not have to wait a month but if you want to complete sooner you will have to give your solicitor plenty of notice. You may, for example, be a first-time buyer, with no property to sell and you may be buying an empty property. In this case, you might as well move in as soon as possible – an empty property is a vulnerable property.

APPOINTING A SURVEYOR

You should also try to find your surveyor by personal recommendation. You want a member of the Royal Institution of Chartered Surveyors with an FRICS or an ARICS after his or her name. Another equally acceptable alternative is a member of the Incorporated Society of Valuers and Auctioneers – an ISVA.

You can ask your surveyor to supply you with a valuation, a house buyer's report or a full structural survey. A valuation, which costs from less than 0.1 per cent to 0.25 per cent of the house price, will be required by your mortgage lender. A house buyer's report costs about double, and will highlight any major defects in the house or flat, stopping short of structural problems, drains, brickwork and woodwork. It is more elaborate and can be carried out by your surveyor at the same time as your valuation.

You get what you pay for – the only completely satisfactory answer with an old house or flat is a full structural survey incorporating the valuation. This way you obtain a definite fix on any work that may need doing, together with full details of any structural defects. The cost is about 0.5 per cent of the value, but nowadays all fees are negotiable, especially for larger houses. Full structural surveys are expensive and may seem to be a 'waste' of money if nothing untoward is found. On the other hand, a full survey may uncover serious faults which make you decide to withdraw from the purchase, in which case the cost of the survey will be money very well spent. Be sure to ask the lender or your mortgage broker if the surveyor you use is on the lender's panel of approved surveyors. You should be able to negotiate a discount if your survey is done at the same time as the compulsory valuation for mortgage purposes.

At the time of writing, the government is proposing legislation which would require a seller to provide a 'seller's pack'. The aim is to speed up the process of buying and selling property. Part of the pack will include a survey. It remains to be seen how this new system works in practice. It may well be that many buyers will still want to arrange their own survey.

FURTHER PRICE NEGOTIATION

Let us return to the hypothetical flat you are buying for the negotiated price of, say, £77,500 and assume that you have just paid about £400 for a full structural survey. The surveyor's report might show that the roof is in a terrible state of repair and needs £2,500 to be spent to make it safe and rainproof. You should now use the surveyor's report to chip at least £2,500, and preferably more, off the price of £77,500 you had previously agreed *subject to survey and contract*.

The surveyor's report can and usually does pay for itself in this way and will also give you a firm idea of the repairs you will need to do if you proceed with the purchase. In the unlikely event that the house is given a clean bill of health, look upon the surveyor's fees as a kind of insurance policy – wonderful to know that you are buying a completely sound house.

WORTH THE HEARTACHE

Condensed into one short chapter, buying a house or flat sounds a lot simpler than it is in reality. Moving house is usually ranked with death and divorce as one of the three most traumatic events of our lives.

However, for anyone with serious financial ambitions, it is absolutely vital that you buy your own home. The key point about property is that you have to live somewhere. It is silly not to use where you live as an important element of your bid to become a millionaire and achieve financial freedom.

The second key element is the way you finance your house or flat purchase. We show you how to do this in the next chapter.

SUMMARY

1. It has paid to be an owner of one's own home during the past century. Property prices have beaten consumer inflation by a wide margin and in our view this trend is likely to continue. Buying your own home well is a vital component of any serious bid to become a millionaire.

2. The property market is a little heady at the moment so proceed with caution. There are a number of key points to consider:

a) Position is the key factor, far more important than condition.

b) Use a checklist to remember crucial points.

c) First do a common sense survey using the suggested checklist supplemented by your own key points.

d) Negotiate toughly, letting the other party make most of the running.

e) Any offer you make should always be subject to contract and subject to survey.

f) Use the criticisms in the survey to lower the suggested purchase price by negotiation.

3. The kind of mortgage you obtain is crucially important as you will see in the next chapter.

4

HOW TO FINANCE YOUR HOME

'If there is anyone listening to whom I owe money, I'm prepared to forget it if you are.'

Errol Flynn

A home loan based on an Individual Savings Account, which is tax-efficient and also enables you to invest in the stock market, is a wonderfully attractive way of funding your house purchase and a key element of your bid to become a millionaire. Endowment mortgages are only good for people selling them and should be avoided like the plague.

Most people buying their own home fund a large part of the purchase price with a mortgage, which is a long-term loan paid back over a period of time. Traditionally, repayment was by monthly instalments including both capital and interest but during the 1980s it became more usual to pay only interest for the duration of the loan and then to repay the full amount with the proceeds of a savings plan.

Your house or flat is pledged as security for the loan and, if you fail to repay it, there is a real chance you will lose your home. It is vital, therefore, that you fund your house purchase sensibly.

The other reason why it is crucial to structure your mortgage correctly is that the way you repay your home loan can be a key element in your bid to become a millionaire and achieve financial freedom. Getting the right kind of mortgage will allow you to benefit fully from the growth of two wonderful financial assets – property and shares.

BEWILDERING CHOICE

Provided you earn enough and have no bad debt record, you will be offered an unimaginably difficult choice of home loans, with all kinds of special offers that cut your costs with one hand and take your money back with the other. One lender alone may offer you as many as 15 different options, including fixed rates for differing periods and various first-time buyer and large loan discounts.

Most borrowers are confused by the complications and jargon which has resulted in few people realising the appalling value they have received from products such as endowment policies. When you consider that the majority of the adult population faces the problem of buying and financing their home, the lack of transparency is a national scandal on a par with the pensions mis-selling fiasco.

CUTTING THROUGH THE JARGON

Mortgages are actually very simple. They have three elements:

1. You borrow an amount of money on which you pay interest. You can choose between paying a rate of interest which rises and falls in line with base rates or one which is fixed or capped for a period of time.

2. You are obviously required to repay the loan at some point. There are two main ways of doing this. Either you pay a small part of the loan each month in addition to your interest payment or you save separately over a number of years and pay off the whole loan in one go.

3. You are very likely to have an insurance policy to ensure that the loan will be paid off if you die before you have finished repaying it.

That is all there is to mortgages. Most people are confused because these three elements are intermingled. For example, with an endowment mortgage the savings vehicle is wrapped up with the life insurance policy, making it almost impossible to see how well (or should we say badly) *your money* is being invested. Think of each of these three key ingredients in isolation from the other two and you are much less likely to be confused and short-changed.

THE LOAN

First, let us deal with the loan. We will show you the full range of mortgage loans currently on offer (at the time of writing) before showing you which are the best.

Types of Loan

Variable rate

Fixed rate

Capped rate

Cap and collar rate

First-time buyer's discount

Cash back

The traditional loan is at a *variable rate* of interest. With this you pay a rate of interest which is pitched slightly above the bank base rate. If interest rates go up, so does your monthly payment to your lender. If interest rates rise sharply, as they did in the late 1980s, this can be very painful and, in the most extreme cases, can mean you are unable to keep up your interest payments and may ultimately lose your home. Of course, when interest rates are falling a variable rate loan is a thing of beauty.

More common these days are *fixed-rate* loans. At present, lenders are competing very hard for business and there is a plethora of fixed-rate low-priced deals. With all of them, the fixed-rate period lasts for a limited time, sometimes only one or two years, and there are always conditions attached, such as penalties for early redemption. Often, high early redemption penalties last for longer than the fixed rate. For example, a two-year fixed rate may carry high redemption penalties for five years but this is not always made clear to borrowers. Also, borrowers may have to take out expensive insurance policies (sometimes household and sometimes life) with the lender and pay higher than usual arrangement fees before they are allowed a special-offer loan. Early in 2002, the basic variable-rate mortgage costs around 4.75 per cent and the cheapest fixed-rate loan from a larger building society is 2.9 per cent, fixed for two years from Northern Rock. At the same time, longer term fixed rates for periods of five years or more are around the 5.4 to 6.0 per cent mark.

The fixed loans could be expensive if rates, which admittedly look like rising later in 2002, stay at today's historically low levels. To help overcome the uncertainty of fluctuating rates, some lenders offer *capped rates* where the interest rate is variable, but guaranteed not to rise above a certain figure. They also offer *cap-and-collar* loans, where the interest rate can move but must stay within a certain range for a specified period. You should always check the exact terms; a cap may mean that interest above a certain level is simply deferred and added to the outstanding capital you owe.

Other special offers include a *first-time buyer's discount* which is only offered on variable rate mortgages. It might, for example, be a 2 per cent discount on the normal variable rate for a two-year period and will usually be accompanied by a lock-in period of about five years. During this period you are obliged to borrow at the variable rate, and early redemptions are heavily penalised.

A recent innovation is a *cash-back mortgage* which usually carries interest at the standard variable rate and offers the borrower a sum of cash, from about £3,000 to £5,000 or more, which can be used at the borrower's discretion. Once again, though, there is a long lock-in period. Don't be misled by seemingly attractive offers – lenders get their money back one way or another.

Which loan to choose?

Deciding which type of loan is best for you is a judgement call on the future direction of interest rates. If you believe interest rates are likely to fall it obviously makes no sense to fix your mortgage at close to the prevailing rate. If you think there is a good chance that inflation is brewing and interest rates will have to rise to choke off rising prices you would not want to be exposed to a variable rate.

Capped rates are often appealing because they provide the certainty that the amount you have to pay each month will not rise to an unaffordable level while leaving open the possibility that you will benefit from falling rates.

It is, of course, possible to have a mix of different

mortgages running at the same time as a kind of hedge against an unexpected move in either direction.

METHODS OF REPAYING A MORTGAGE

Once you have decided on the type of loan you want to take out, you have to turn your attention to how to pay off the debt. If you thought there was a bewildering variety of loans available, just wait till you see how you can repay your borrowings.

Types of Repayment Method

Traditional capital repayment

Flexible capital repayment

Full with-profits endowment

Low-cost with-profits endowment

Low-start endowment

Unit-linked endowment

Unitised with-profits endowment

Pension-linked

Individual Savings Account (ISA)

As we have seen, these fall into two main categories – regular capital repayments and savings plans to fund a one-off repayment after several years. First let us examine the regular repayment methods:

Traditional capital repayment

This is how mortgages used to be. Each month you pay interest and repay a small part of the capital until, after twenty-five years or so, you have paid back the entire sum. They have the great virtue of simplicity.

Flexible capital repayment

The latest fashion in mortgages is the flexible mortgage, also called the Australian mortgage because it originated in Australia and has become the norm there. It looks as though it could also become popular in the UK. A truly flexible mortgage has some interesting characteristics – interest is charged daily rather than monthly or annually. Daily charging means that any capital repayment into your mortgage account *immediately* reduces the outstanding balance on which interest is charged. If you are allowed to make overpayments whenever you can afford them, you can reduce the interest charges and perhaps pay off the mortgage much sooner than you originally planned. As the chart opposite shows, being able to make overpayments can save you a great deal of money over the years.

A flexible mortgage also allows you to make under-payments or miss monthly payments, sometimes within strict limits. Furthermore, you may be able to re-borrow money already paid back or borrow extra money up to a certain limit if you need a loan, for example to buy a car. In fact you may be able to put all your borrowing require-ments on to the mortgage. This is advantageous if you tend to use credit cards and personal loans, because mortgage interest rates are usually much lower than credit card and personal loan rates.

A few flexible mortgage accounts can act as all-purpose accounts, replacing separate current, credit card, personal loan and mortgage accounts. Some lenders are dipping their toes rather cautiously into the flexible mortgage market and their loans are not as flexible as others so, if the idea appeals to you, you need to shop around for the right one.

Benefit of Regular Overpayment

	Using 7.0% payment		Payment + £50 a month	
	Bal B/fwd	Interest	Bal B/fwd	Interest
	(£)		(£)	
YR1	98,601.78	6,951.53	98,035.46	6,931.90
YR2	96,970.89	6,840.94	95,744.01	6,776.54
YR3	95,222.09	6,722.35	93,286.92	6,609.92
YR4	93,346.87	6,595.19	90,652.19	6,431.25
YR5	91,336.10	6,458.85	87,826.99	6,239.67
YR6	89,179.96	6,312.64	84,797.55	6,034.24
YR7	86,867.96	6,155.86	81,549.72	5,813.97
YR8	84,388.84	5,987.77	78,065.86	5,577.77
YR9	81,500.48	6,282.92	74,007.62	5,756.22
YR10	78,385.24	6,054.72	69,630.61	5,435.59
YR11	75,292.89	5,370.96	65,285.77	4,711.16
YR12	71,977.00	5,146.12	60,626.82	4,395.23
YR13	68,421.41	4,905.01	55,631.08	4,056.46
YR14	64,608.78	4,646.48	50,274.20	3,693.23
YR15	60,520.54	4,369.27	44,530.08	3,303.72
YR16	56,136.75	4,071.99	38,370.71	2,886.06
YR17	51,436.06	3,753.24	31,766.07	2,438.18
YR18	46,395.53	3,411.42	24,683.99	1,957.96
YR19	40,990.64	3,044.93	17,089.96	1,443.02
YR20	35,195.02	2,651.92	8,946.95	890.84
YR21	28,980.45	2,230.53	215.28	298.75
YR22	22,316.63	1,778.66	Nil	Nil
YR23	15,171.08	1,294.12		
YR24	7,508.97	774.54		
YR25	Nil	221.55		

Total interest paid £112,033.51   Total interest paid £91,681.68

Capital repayment mortgage = £100,000

Normal monthly payment = £693.12

Source: Abbey National

The biggest downside of the flexible loan is the interest rate, which tends to be either the lender's standard variable rate or base rate plus one percentage point – 4.75 to 5.0 per cent early in 2002. It may be worth paying their rate if you want to take full advantage of the flexible options. However, if you are unlikely to use them, you may be better off going for a good fixed-rate deal with all its inflexibilities. The other possible downside – especially with the fully flexible, current account mortgage – is that you may be treading water forever by constantly borrowing up to your limit and never reducing your debt. You need to be disciplined with this kind of mortgage.

Now let us turn our attention to savings-backed interest-only mortgages:

Full with-profits endowment

In the 1970s, with-profits endowment life insurance policies started to be sold with mortgages. Each month, you repay the interest element to the lender and premiums on the life policy to an insurance company; the policy pays out on death or the date the loan is due to be repaid.

Lenders and brokers like endowment mortgages because they earn hefty commissions selling them on behalf of insurance companies. However, since 1984 there has been no tax relief on life insurance premiums and the attractions for borrowers today are very limited indeed.

Low-cost with-profits endowment

Full with-profits endowment mortgages were expensive, so the next stage was the low-cost and/or low-start with-profits endowment mortgages. Regrettably these are still sold today although a growing number of lenders have stopped offering endowment-backed loans. Because the final payout on a full with-profits endowment mortgage was usually far more than was needed to meet the debt, lenders began to allow borrowers to take an increasingly aggressive position based on overly optimistic projected rates of growth. They also made the unsafe assumption that the annual bonuses and terminal bonus added to the basic sum assured would be more than enough to repay the debt.

In the past few years, with-profits bonuses have fallen. There is now a strong possibility that someone who has taken out a low-cost with-profits endowment might not receive enough money from the policy when the mortgage is due to be repaid and many people have received distressing letters telling them that their policies are unlikely to pay off their mortgage on the due date.

These people can stick with their policies and increase their premiums but we believe that they should instead face up to the basic problem that entering into the original endowment policy may have been a mistake. They should consider surrendering their policies and switching to a self-administered ISA savings plan. In the next chapter, we explain how to decide whether to surrender an endowment and how to do so.

Low-start endowment

Low-start policies are another kind of add-on option to the range of endowments on offer. They were designed to enable borrowers to pay less in the early years, generally working on the basis of increasing premiums by 10–20 per cent a year for a fixed period. Like low-cost policies, they can be either with-profits or unit-linked.

Unit-linked endowment

During the 1980s, unit-linked life insurance policies became more widely used for repaying mortgages. Unit-linked policies are riskier as they relate directly to movements in the stock market. As the old adage goes, the value of your investments can go down as well as up.

When you invest for the *very long term* with a unit-linked policy, provided you do not cash it in early, you can be reasonably confident that your money will grow substantially and the proceeds should be more than enough to pay off your mortgage.

Unitised with-profits endowment

More recently, with-profits policies have become less available as the insurance companies have converted to selling unitised with-profits policies, a hybrid between traditional with-profits and unit-linked policies which is less expensive for the insurer. They are less risky than traditional with-profits and unit-linked policies because the value of the units cannot go down as bonuses are locked in each year.

Pension-linked

Lenders are relaxed about accepting life policies as collateral because they know they can usually sell the underlying property for a profit to reclaim their money. For the same reason, many are happy to allow borrowers to save in personal pension schemes to repay the loan. Lenders do not usually ask for security to be assigned nowadays, not even with endowment policies.

A pension-linked mortgage is tax-efficient because there is tax relief on pension contributions which can then be invested in a tax-free fund. As a consequence, the net monthly payments you need to make are lower than for a comparable endowment policy. Pension fund investments can also grow much faster than endowment policies because they pay no tax on certain types of investment income (deposits and bonds) or capital gains.

But there are drawbacks. Because 75 per cent of your pension fund *must* be used to buy an annuity, you will have to use the bulk or all of the remaining tax-free lump sum from your pension on retirement to repay your mortgage. This will restrict your option to take a smaller lump sum, which you may want to do, so that you can buy a bigger annuity. Furthermore, pension-linked mortgages are very inflexible. If you are young, you could end up paying interest on the mortgage for a great deal longer than 25 years. Also, you should not rule out the possibility that, at a later stage in your career, you may want to join a company pension scheme. This could be complicated and, if it happened, you would need to obtain expert advice.

ISA

Individual Savings Accounts (ISAs) – like their predecessors, Personal Equity Plans, or PEPs – have become acceptable as tax-efficient savings schemes linked to mortgages. An ISA is extremely tax-efficient; there is no tax on capital gains on shares and bonds and no tax on the income from cash and bond investments within the plan. The plan manager can reclaim a 10 per cent tax credit on share dividends until April 2004. In addition, higher-rate taxpayers avoid the extra tax they would have to pay on dividends on shares and share-based investments held outside an ISA.

ISAs are also more flexible than other interest-only mortgage repayment methods as you are not locked in for a set period and you can choose from a wide variety of investments to suit your temperament.

ISA mortgages pay a very small commission compared with unit-linked endowments, with-profits endowments and pension-linked mortgages, so do not expect commission-based advisers to be enthusiastic about them. Their advantages will be explained later.

CHOOSING YOUR REPAYMENT METHOD

Now that you have some appreciation of the range of repayment methods on offer, it is time to sort the wheat from the chaff.

The most basic point to grasp is that endowment policies are to be avoided like the plague. They provide poor investment returns and confuse what should be a simple issue. If you are borrowing a large amount of money to buy a home, you want to repay as much as you can reasonably afford each month to be sure of repaying the capital sum on the due date. Meanwhile, if you have any dependants you will almost certainly want to insure your life so that if you die prematurely the mortgage will be paid off in full. However, these are separate issues and should be treated as such. We do not recommend giving even a second thought to endowment policies. They are structured so that substantial commissions can be paid and they may not provide sufficient capital profits for borrowers to repay their mortgages. There are much better options available.

You might well ask why so many endowment policies have been sold. The answer is that there used to be tax advantages, the industry has become very used to them and, perhaps most important of all, the brokers and lenders who place endowment policies have received very fat commissions. These commissions cost you, the borrower, money, most noticeably and painfully if you try to surrender your policy in the early years.

The second important point to realise is that it is never too late to put your financial affairs in order. If you are already committed to an endowment policy, you can and in many cases should change to a more effective method of repaying your mortgage. The pros and cons are dealt with very fully in the next chapter.

The third point to understand is that if you want to become a millionaire it is essential to fund the purchase of your home in a *way that allows you to invest tax-efficiently in the stock market in parallel with the investment in your property*. Pension-linked and ISA mortgages (topped up with PEPs if you have any) are the most efficient way to invest in two wonderful long-term financial assets, property and shares, *at the same time*.

If you do not want to take the additional risk of buying shares as well as buying your own home, you should simply fund the purchase of the property you buy with a traditional capital repayment mortgage or a flexible capital repayment mortgage. Perhaps at a later stage in your life, you can then buy another property to let and try to make your million that way. However, by the time you have finished reading this book we are confident you will conclude that shares, purchased systematically, can be 'safer than houses'. Unlike a second property, your capital gains from the shares will also be completely free of tax if you use ISAs.

PENSION OR ISA?

The choice between a pension mortgage and an ISA mortgage is not clear cut. A pension mortgage is attractive because the yearly contributions are allowable for taxation. A higher-rate tax payer can invest £100 a month by contributing only £60 of after-tax income. With an ISA the contributions are not allowable but all of the funds are free of tax when it comes to repayment in contrast to just the lump sum from a pension fund, which is usually limited to 25 per cent of the funds available.

Both pension-linked and ISA funds pay no capital gains tax while the funds accumulate, but a pension mortgage is definitely more inflexible as you are locked in for a very long period. Also, with a pension mortgage, after you have received the lump sum you can be *compelled* at the age of 75 to buy a taxable annuity. With current low interest rates and increased life expectancy, annuities are very expensive indeed. In contrast, if you use ISAs, both to pay off your mortgage and to provide your retirement income, you can receive a tax-free income for life. A far better return can be made by keeping control of your own capital and putting it to work in the stock market. When you die your descendants can also then inherit the capital sum. *On balance, an ISA mortgage is to be preferred to a pension mortgage* but the decision is quite a close one. Certainly, for the purposes of most readers of this book who intend to become millionaires, an ISA mortgage is the answer.

Straightforward repayment, ISA and pension mortgages are a far better proposition than endowment mortgages. Fortunately, it is not so hard these days to find a building society or bank to meet your requirements. Some of the big ones have already bowed to public and media pressure and stopped selling endowment mortgages. If you want an

ISA mortgage or a straightforward capital repayment mortgage, *insist* on it. You may still encounter resistance and have obstacles put in your way like losing the benefit of any special rates on offer. Whatever the problems, remain resolute – getting the right kind of mortgage established is an absolutely crucial decision for you.

DIY or IFA?

If you are prepared to put in the groundwork yourself, you can simply go straight to your bank and/or your nearest building society and find out exactly what they have on offer. The whole subject of mortgages is a very complex one, however, so most people feel happier with expert professional advice. There is a lot to be said for seeing an *independent* adviser who knows all the products on offer and can shop around on your behalf for the most competitive and suitable one. However, you should always ascertain at the outset if the advisers have products that meet your requirements. They may, for example, be unable to offer repayment or ISA mortgages in which case *you must go elsewhere.* You should also establish how much their advice will cost you and *exactly* how they expect to be remunerated. They are compelled to tell you.

HOW MUCH TO SAVE IN YOUR ISA?

Having decided to repay your mortgage with the proceeds of an ISA savings plan, the final important decision is how much you will need to contribute to ensure you can repay your loan in good time.

It makes sense to take advice on this because if you underestimate the required contributions, or you are too optimistic about the rate at which you can grow your savings, you could find yourself at your chosen repayment date with an insufficient fund. You need to make conservative assumptions about the rate of return you are likely to achieve and be realistic about the length of time you want to remain committed to making regular contributions.

To help you calculate how much you need to save we have compiled a ready reckoner which shows you the size of fund you can expect to achieve on the basis of a variety of assumptions.

The table below shows what you could expect to achieve if you were to contribute £1,000 a year into your fund, investing once a year at the end of each year. Choosing an appropriate time period and rate of return will show you how much your final fund will be worth. For example, if you want to pay off your mortgage in 18 years' time and believe you will achieve a compound rate of return of 12 per cent you will be able to turn £1,000 a year, or around £83 a month, into £55,750. If you propose to borrow twice as much as this, an £111,500 mortgage, and repay it after the same 18-year period, you will need to save twice as much, £2,000 a year or £167 a month.

Repaying your Mortgage

£1000 pa premium	6%	9%	12%	15%	18%
3 years	3,184	3,278	3,374	3,473	3,572
6 years	6,975	7,523	8,115	8,754	9,442
9 years	11,491	13,021	14,776	16,786	19,086
12 years	16,870	20,141	24,133	29,002	34,931
15 years	23,276	29,361	37,280	47,580	60,965
18 years	30,906	41,301	55,750	75,836	103,740
21 years	39,993	56,765	81,699	118,810	174,021
24 years	50,816	76,789	118,155	184,168	289,494

Obviously, if you want to repay your mortgage over a shorter period you will need either to achieve a higher rate of return or to save more. *Be very careful – it is much better to save more than you think you will need than to assume a higher rate of return. You will find a way to spend any surplus, but making up any shortfall may be very painful indeed.*

SECURE FOUNDATIONS

This chapter and the previous one show you how to put the groundwork in place for your bid to become a millionaire. You will have bought your own house or flat and financed the mortgage on it with an ISA savings plan. This is the way to benefit from the miraculous compounding of two wonderful financial assets, property and shares.

If you are now in this lucky position skip ahead to Chapter 6 for the second half of the blueprint for financial success. However, many people cannot immediately launch their bid for financial freedom in this sensible way because they are already saddled with an inappropriate endowment policy. If you are in this unfortunate position do not worry unduly – it is rarely too late to put your financial house in order. You will, however, need to undertake some remedial action and the next chapter offers a range of possible solutions.

SUMMARY

Obtain the maximum mortgage you can afford, bearing in mind the following points:

1. Keep the three elements of a mortgage separate in your mind.

    a) First, you want to borrow money as cheaply as possible.
    b) Second, you want to repay your borrowings as quickly and tax-efficiently as possible.
    c) Finally, you will probably want to make sure that your life is adequately insured so that your dependants are not left with an unpaid loan should you die early.

2. Lenders want your business. Remember that special deals are often not so special when you examine them more closely.

3. Mortgages linked to endowment policies, whether with-profits or unit-linked, are very unattractive indeed. They only offer minimal tax advantages for those who pay higher-rate tax and who regularly use up their annual capital gains tax allowance. However, salesmen receive such large commissions for selling endowment policies, that even these minor advantages can be negated. One way or another, the borrower always ends up paying and there is then less money available to repay your mortgage or give you a worthwhile surrender value.

4. If you already have an endowment policy *consider surrendering it immediately and switching to an ISA mortgage.* The implications of doing this are outlined in detail in the next chapter.

5. If you do not want to take the extra risk of investing in the stock market as well as your home, you should consider a traditional capital repayment mortgage or a flexible repayment mortgage. With a capital repayment

mortgage you know exactly where you stand and, provided you can keep up your monthly payments, you know for certain that your mortgage will be repaid at the end of the period.

6. There are substantial tax advantages with pension mortgages. They usually result in lower monthly payments than endowment policies.

7. ISA mortgages are very tax-efficient and enable you to invest in the stock market as well as in your own home. They are the right answer for anyone with serious financial ambitions.

8. You can do the groundwork yourself and choose the mortgage that best suits your requirements. Mortgages are complex, however, and many people feel happier taking expert independent advice.

9. Use the table to calculate how much you need to save in order to pay back your mortgage at your chosen date. Be very conservative in your assumptions.

10. If you are starting out, skip to Chapter 6 for the next stage in the blueprint for financial success. If, however, you are unable to immediately start an ISA mortgage because you are already saddled with an endowment, Chapter 5 offers a range of solutions.

5

REVIEW YOUR ENDOWMENTS

'Money is better than poverty, if only for financial reasons.'

Woody Allen

When you make your first flat or house purchase, do not give a second thought to an endowment policy. If you are already on the housing ladder and find yourself saddled with one, calculate whether you should surrender or sell your policy and use the proceeds to start an ISA savings plan.

CONFIRMING OUR WORST FEARS

If we had any lingering doubts that endowments should be avoided like the plague, our minds were put at rest when we had sight recently of one of the hundreds of thousands of letters sent by insurance companies to many of the holders of their policies. The letter made crystal clear why endowments are rapidly being abandoned as a method of repaying mortgages.

The policy holder, a 36-year-old man, had entered into an endowment policy exactly 10 years earlier in order to pay back the £74,000 loan he had taken out to buy his flat. The details of the policy were as follows:

Term: 25 years
Premium: £97.59 a month
Guaranteed death benefit: £74,000

The letter advised the policy holder – we will call him Bill – that far from paying off his £74,000 mortgage, the policy was now expected to fall more than £17,500 short of the required sum. Here is the relevant passage:

'To arrive at the estimated maturity value we have taken a long term view of the investment outlook. We have assumed a suitable growth rate, that all premiums are paid when due and then projected the basic sum assured plus attaching bonuses to the end of your policy term. For the purposes of this review we believe 6.00 per cent per annum to be a reasonable assumption for a fixed rate of future investment return.

'Having conducted this review, the current estimated maturity value of your policy is £17,576 less than the guaranteed death benefit.'

You can imagine how Bill felt, reading this letter. He was aware that the stock market was close to its all time high. Over the 10 years since his policy was taken out, the market had enjoyed one of the longest bull runs in history. Not surprisingly, Bill did some back-of-envelope calculations to try to understand why an apparently safe method of saving to pay off his mortgage had come so badly unstuck. He was familiar with the wonderful power of compounding and was, therefore, puzzled that a company employing highly-paid professional investors believed it was only capable of turning premiums paid of £29,250 into £56,424 *over 25 years*.

POOR PERFORMANCE

The results of Bill's calculations were sobering reading. They suggested that the household name to whom he had entrusted his savings had done an indifferent job of investing his money during the first 10 years of the policy and was forecasting more of the same lacklustre performance for the remaining 15.

At £97.59 every month, Bill calculated that he had paid just over £1,170 a year into his endowment policy. Looking up term insurance rates on a personal finance website, he calculated that no more than £170 of this could have been accounted for by the life insurance element of the policy. In fact, his research showed that, today, a 35-year-old man could buy £100,000 of term insurance lasting 20 years for £10 a month, only £120 a year. Also, he was 26 when he took out the policy so it would have been even cheaper to insure his life then. Stripping the £170 a year out of his contributions left £1,000 a year as the assumed savings element of the endowment. Bill calculated that if the insurance company were to achieve an annual growth rate of only 10 per cent after charges over the 25 years of the policy he would receive over £98,000 at the end of the term, over 70 per cent more than he was now being promised.

Remember, 10 per cent is much less than the average total return from the stock market over the past 20 years, not a very demanding target for a professional investor.

Were the insurer to achieve 15 per cent, Bill calculated, he could look forward to £213,000 after 25 years. His £74,000 mortgage would be repaid with ease and he would also enjoy a sizeable lump sum.

To turn Bill's £1,000 a year contributions into £74,000 and simply pay off the mortgage loan, the insurer would have to achieve a return of only 8 per cent a year, around half the market average total return in recent years. Even this meagre target was too ambitious for them.

WEIGHING UP THE OPTIONS

Concerned by his findings, Bill began to investigate his options. The first of these was to take out another, shorter policy to make up the projected shortfall. This was unattractive – a clear case of pouring good money after bad. To Bill, it would feel like rewarding the insurance company for managing his money so badly.

The second option was to take over the investment of the money himself. As a first step Bill contacted the insurer to ascertain the surrender value of the policy, even though he knew that this was likely to be a derisory amount because of the high level of up-front charges levied on this kind of policy and the way in which a very large part of the value of endowments is held back until maturity when a terminal bonus is paid out.

Sure enough, the surrender value was only marginally more than the amount Bill had contributed to the investment element of his policy. At £1,000 a year, excluding the £170 a year life insurance element, Bill calculated that he had paid £10,000 into his policy for investment. The surrender after ten years was a meagre £11,000.

Bill then worked through a range of scenarios – with each, he started with £11,000, applied a fixed rate of return for each of the remaining 15 years and assumed that he would continue contributing the £1,000 a year he was currently paying in premiums. The results of his calculations were encouraging.

Bill found that if he were able to achieve just a 10 per cent investment return on average over the next 15 years, he would be able to turn his £11,000, with the £1,000 annual increments, into £70,000. He would make almost enough to pay off the mortgage and would certainly come a great deal closer than was likely if the insurance company's projection proved correct. Remember, the letter had warned him that the insurance company believed it would achieve only £56,424 by the end of the policy term.

Assuming a better average rate of return of 15 per cent, the picture looked much brighter. Achieving this would turn the £11,000 into £118,000 over the same period. Bill would be able to pay off his mortgage and be left with a meaningful lump sum at the end.

ENHANCING THE SURRENDER VALUE

Even though Bill would be starting with the insurance company's poor surrender value, he calculated that he would not have to produce an unrealistic investment performance over the remaining 15 years to outperform the professionals. This is because, thanks to the power of compounding, even a relatively small annual out-performance can make a very substantial difference over a number of years. Bill was inclining towards taking over the investment of his savings, but his investigations were not yet complete.

A search of the internet brought to his attention the Association of Policy Market Makers (APMM). The APMM's member firms buy and sell with-profits endowment and whole of life policies. All its members are authorised by the Personal Investment Authority, they adhere to practice guidelines and are protected by profes-sional indemnity insurance. The main purpose of the APMM is to provide the framework for an orderly market in traded policies.

When Bill looked at the APMM website (www.moneyextra.co.uk/apmm) there were eight member firms listed. One of these, Foster & Cranfield, was an auctioneer of policies. The others were all market-makers, who act as a principal in buying policies on their own account rather than as brokers.

Bill contacted all eight firms to get quotations for his policy. In the case of the auction house, this was an estimate of the likely proceeds of a sale. The market-makers, on the other hand, were able to make a firm offer, which was valid for a period of between one and two weeks from the date of their offer.

SELLING THE POLICY

Dealing with a market-maker for an endowment policy is the simplest option, other than straight surrender, because right from the outset you know how much you will receive. As you are entering into an agreement with only one other party there is also less potential for the deal to fall through. With an auction, it is possible that your reserve price will not be met and the policy could remain unsold.

Market-makers are able to offer more than the insurance companies' surrender values because the intrinsic value of a policy is higher than the surrender value to a long-term investor who is prepared to continue paying the premiums for the remainder of the term and benefit from all the bonuses including the large terminal bonus. A 25-year policy with 10 years already elapsed might seem to be attractive to someone with a small lump sum to invest who knows that in 15 years' time they will need a substantial larger sum for the university education of a child, for example.

Bill received a range of quotations for his policy. Not all the firms were interested in buying it and others offered a wide variety of prices so it was worth shopping around. Quotations can be requested over the phone which makes the research a relatively easy task and well worth a couple of hours' work.

The best offer Bill received was for £11,796, which was £800 more than the insurance company had quoted for surrender. While this does not sound a massive enhancement, Bill calculated that investing the £800 at 15 per cent over the remaining 15-year period would turn it into a £6,500 improvement on the final value of his fund. Well worth a little extra paperwork.

Most of the market-makers told Bill that they were unable to better the surrender value he had been offered by the insurance company. This was disappointing, but it also confirmed that he was at least receiving close to the market value of his policy.

HOW TO SELL AN ENDOWMENT

Different market makers have slightly varying procedures but they all follow the same broad approach. If you want to proceed with an offer you must sign and return the offer letter, which commits you to the sale. You must also sign an authority to release information, which enables the purchaser of your policy to confirm its details with the insurance company.

The next stage is to send the policy document to the buyer. Sometimes, this will be held by your mortgage lender as security for the loan, but these days this is not usually the case. You may have to ask your lender to write you a letter, saying it no longer has an interest in the policy.

The buyer also needs to see proof of your age, so you will be required to send your passport or birth certificate.

If your name has changed through marriage, you will also need to confirm this by sending your marriage certificate. These documents will usually be returned by Recorded Delivery.

Once confirmed, the market maker will send you a Deed of Assignment and a Referees form. The assignment transfers ownership to the purchaser and should be signed and witnessed by a professional person such as a broker or solicitor. Finally, when all documents have been received, the market maker will send you a cheque and you can begin investing the proceeds.

Although this process is more complicated than simply surrendering the policy, it is a relatively small price to pay for the extra amount you are likely to receive. When weighing up whether to sell or surrender, remember to calculate what the extra amount will be worth over the period of the policy. Thanks to the wonderful power of compounding, it will certainly be many times greater than at the outset.

AUCTIONING THE POLICY

Before reaching his final decision, Bill also investigated the possibility of auctioning the policy through the one auction house on the APMM list. He contacted Foster & Cranfield, which claims to realise millions of pounds for policy holders every month, operating on a 'no sale no fee' basis. The firm believes it can usually achieve up to 15 per cent more than surrender values when it sells policies.

In this case, Foster & Cranfield told Bill that it might expect to raise between £11,500 and £12,250 for the policy. At the top of the range, this was broadly in line with the best quote he received from a market-maker because Foster & Cranfield would charge a fee of £50 plus a third of the difference between the quoted surrender value and the amount achieved in the auction. As the outcome of an auction was uncertain, a straight sale was *in this instance* the preferable option, but each policy is different so it is always worth getting a full range of quotations.

HOW AN AUCTION WORKS

Selling an endowment policy at auction is not complicated. Having obtained an estimate from the auctioneer and decided to proceed, all you have to do is send a letter of authority to sell the policy, indicating the policy number and a reserve price below which you are not prepared to sell. You also have to confirm that you are in possession of the original policy document and warrant that you have paid all the premiums to date.

Once you have filled in this authority to sell, you simply send it with a copy of the policy document, a copy of the latest bonus notice and a written surrender quote from the insurance company and wait for the next auction. These are held once or twice a week.

When the policy is sold, the auctioneer will send you a deed of assignment. You have to pay the premiums up to the date of completion to make sure the policy does not lapse. Completion normally takes place 28 days after the sale, provided you have supplied all the required documents.

WHO SHOULD CONSIDER SURRENDERING?

It is not possible to generalise about who should consider surrendering an endowment policy and switching to a self-administered investment scheme. We believe that for many people saddled with endowments the simple arithmetic of compound interest provides a compelling reason to bite the bullet. However, it is obviously essential to be extremely conservative in your assumptions.

The decision on whether you should stick with your endowment or should surrender or sell it depends on three main factors – first, the size of the surrender value or likely proceeds of a sale or auction of your policy; second, the feasibility of you achieving the required rate of return after charges and tax to do better over the remaining term than the insurance company is likely to achieve; finally, the degree of risk with which you feel comfortable.

This last point refers to the fact that to give yourself the best chance of beating the investment performance of the insurance company you should invest only in shares rather than the mixture of assets favoured by most endowment funds. This sort of investment approach is not considered appropriate for people who are 'risk-averse', although the Barclays study clearly demonstrates that in the long run, exposure to the stock market in this way is in fact *prudent*.

The other two factors are more mathematical in nature, although they do depend crucially on a judgement and comparison of the future investment returns you and your endowment provider are likely to make. As we have seen, Bill's decision was not a very difficult one because he calculated that, given the size of the surrender value of his policy, he would only need to achieve a relatively low rate of return by historical standards to beat his insurance company. Because his policy had 15 years to run, there was still sufficient time for even a relatively small average annual outperformance to result in a meaningful long-term advantage.

SURRENDERING MORE RECENT POLICIES

The shorter the time you have been paying into an endowment, the more likely it is that you should bite the bullet and surrender the policy. You will probably not even get your premiums back at a very early stage, but the key point is that you will have longer to let the power of compounding weave its magic on the few percentage points of better annual performance you should expect to achieve.

Encouraged by the results of Bill's research, a friend of his, Charles, reassessed his own endowments. Again, the name has been changed, but this is another real example. Like many people, Charles had several policies outstanding, a result of a series of house moves. Each time he traded up to a larger, more expensive property he took out a top-up endowment to cover the extra debt.

The most recent move was only 16 months previously, so this was a relatively new policy. The conventional wisdom, as we have seen, is that it is not worth surrendering this sort of policy because the charging structure means you are unlikely to get back even the premiums you have already paid.

However, what is much more important about a very early surrender such as Charles's is that he is actually in a stronger position because he has wasted less time investing poorly and still has a relatively long period of time in which to allow the power of compounding to get to work on the higher rate of annual return he expects to achieve. The details of Charles's policy are as follows:

Term: 17 years (to coincide with the maturity of an earlier 25 year plan)
Premium: £138.70 a month
Guaranteed death benefit: £46,000

Charles contacted his insurance company and was quoted a surrender value of £728.27. This compared with total premiums paid of £2,219.20, so Charles faced a painful up-front hit. The reason the surrender value was so low was that for the first 27 months of his policy only 60 per cent of his premiums were to be invested on his behalf. *The rest was earmarked for life cover, charges and commission.*

Charles realised, however, that the cost of staying with the policy was likely to be much greater in the long run if his insurance company, like Bill's, failed to achieve more than 6 per cent a year for the 15 years remaining of the policy term.

Visiting the Moneyextra website (www.moneyextra.co.uk), he calculated that he could take out a £100,000 term insurance policy for only £13 a month, more than adequate to cover his life for the £46,000 outstanding loan. Stripping this out from the £138.70 premiums he was currently paying would leave him with £125 a month to invest, £1,500 a year.

Charles then calculated that starting with his £700 surrender value, achieving a return of just 10 per cent a year and adding in £1,500 every 12 months, he would be able to build up a fund worth over £50,000 during the 15-year period.

In other words, using a very conservative rate of return of only a little over half the 20-year average stock market return, Charles would be able to repay his mortgage comfortably.

Using a 15 per cent return, Charles calculated his fund would be worth £77,000, safely more than the £46,000 loan.

As with Bill's policy, which had been in force for 10 years, the early surrender of Charles's 15-month-old policy appeared to make good arithmetical sense.

SURRENDERING CLOSER TO MATURITY

We have made an important assumption so far in this chapter – that the insurance companies will achieve no more than the 6 per cent quoted in the letter from Bill's endowment provider. It should be pointed out that strict rules constrain the projections insurance companies are allowed to make in correspondence with their clients and it is, of course, possible that they will in fact do much better over the next 15 years. It is quite conceivable that they might make 8 per cent or even 10 per cent a year or more.

Standard Life, for example, calculates that its 25-year endowment policies maturing in February 2002 produced a 13 per cent annualised return. A 10-year Standard Life policy maturing at the same date produced a 9.6 per cent return. It would be wrong, therefore, to assume that the 6 per cent the companies are obliged to use for their projections will not be easily beaten, if past performance is any guide.

It is also possible that the 10 per cent and 15 per cent total returns used in Bill's and Charles's personal projections turn out to be too high. If Bill and Charles choose to invest directly in shares, for example, rather than passively through a low-cost tracker fund, they will incur charges every time they buy and sell shares. These might reduce their annual total return by 3 per cent or more.

Moreover, in a period of low inflation and low interest rates, it is quite likely that the average annual total return from the stock market will be lower than the average of recent years.

However, the large difference between the insurers' projections and a target return for an investor of, say, 15 per cent provides a sufficient margin of safety. Neither Bill nor Charles are being foolhardy in assuming that a self-administered, shares-only investment approach stands a very good chance of outperforming their current endowment providers, especially bearing in mind their poor record to date. An important point to bear in mind is that an annual outperformance of only 4 per cent or 5 per cent, after charges and any tax, will make a significant difference over 15 or 20 years. If you are not confident of achieving this superior performance, of course, surrender or sale is not for you but we believe most people can reasonably safely predict a better return.

Another important consideration with both Bill's and Charles's cases is that the surrender or sale proceeds are small enough to be easily sheltered from tax in an ISA. We explain later in detail the mechanics of setting up an ISA and the exact amounts that can be invested each year. Broadly speaking, however, up to £7,000 a year per person can be invested in an ISA which means that Bill would either have to shelter his starting capital over two financial years or use his wife's allowance in addition to his own in the first year. Charles could shelter his entire surrender value at a stroke. It is important that as much as possible of the proceeds are protected by the tax-free wrapper of an ISA. Any portion of the starting fund which is not shielded in this way will have to work much harder because capital gains in excess of the annual tax-free limit will be liable to capital gains tax. For anyone with serious financial ambitions, the annual return in excess of the insurance companies' 6 per cent projection means that, even factoring in a possible tax liability on some future capital gains, the arithmetic still favours surrender. It is, however, another important factor to bear in mind when weighing up the options.

The ability to reclaim in an ISA the 10 per cent tax deducted from dividends will cease in 2004. We have not factored this into our calculations as the net effect is unlikely to be more than 0.5 per cent a year.

The tax factor is one reason why the question of surrender becomes more thorny the longer you have been paying into a policy. If, for example, your surrender value is considerably in excess of the annual ISA allowance, you might find it difficult to shelter the full amount from tax even over several years. This could dramatically reduce the annual return you can expect to make and might tip the scales against surrendering.

The second main reason why the long-term holder of an endowment faces a more difficult choice is because they have so much less time to undo the damage of previous sub-standard investment performance. Because so much of the final payout of an endowment comes in the form of a terminal bonus, a policy holder of say 20 years' standing is still likely to receive a relatively poor surrender value but, crucially, will only have five years left in which to outperform the insurance company.

COMPARE AND CONTRAST

You have nothing to lose and possibly a great deal to gain by requesting a projected fund value and a surrender value from your insurance company. Having done so, take a conservative rate of growth (say 12 per cent, with yearly rests) and work out, using the table opposite how much this will turn your surrender value into over the remaining term. If some of your fund is likely to remain outside the tax shelter of an ISA, you should assume a lower rate of return to allow for the estimated tax charge. Remember that investing your surrender value is only half the equation. You will also be investing the premiums you were paying into your endowment policy into an ISA savings plan. We showed you how to calculate the size of

Lump Sum Investment Returns

£1000	6%	9%	12%	15%	18%
lump sum					
3 years	1,191	1,295	1,405	1,521	1,643
6 years	1,419	1,677	1,974	2,313	2,699
9 years	1,689	2,172	2,773	3,518	4,435
12 years	2,012	2,813	3,896	5,350	7,288
15 years	2,397	3,642	5,474	8,137	11,974
18 years	2,854	4,717	7,689	12,375	19,673
21 years	3,399	6,109	10,804	18,822	32,324
24 years	4,049	7,911	15,178	28,625	53,109

this fund at the end of Chapter 4. Add together the result of investing both your surrender value and your continuing monthly premiums to arrive at your total fund.

When you have made the calculation, compare the result with the insurer's projection. You may well decide that the decision is a close one. In that event it may not be worth while surrendering. But you will at least have the comfort of knowing that you have made a rational choice instead of just sticking with a disadvantageous contract out of ignorance or inertia.

Remember, too, that it is possible to keep one or more older policies running while surrendering younger policies. It does not have to be all or nothing.

SHOULD I SURRENDER MY ENDOWMENT POLICY?

To decide whether or not to proceed with a sale or surrender of your endowment policy you need to compare your insurance company's projection of the likely size of your fund with the amount that you can *realistically* achieve by taking the surrender value and investing it, together with the amount you are currently paying as premiums, for the remainder of the policy's term.

To calculate the size of your investment fund when your mortgage is due to be repaid you need to make two separate calculations and add together the results. First, use the table on page 79 to calculate how much your surrender value will grow assuming the rate of return with which you feel comfortable and applying the appropriate number of years remaining before repayment is due.

All the figures in the table are for a starting value of £1,000 so if, for example, your surrender value is £11,000 you need to multiply the result by eleven.

Second, use the table in Chapter 4 on page 60 to calculate how your continuing premiums will grow over the remaining term until the mortgage is due for repayment. Remember, the table is for an annual premium of £1,000 so if you are currently paying £3,000 into your endowment policy (£250 a month), multiply the appropriate figure by three.

Finally, add together the results of the two calculations. This will be the size of your fund assuming you meet the rate of return you have chosen and continue investing for the whole of the term you have selected.

Example:
Peter has a £7,000 surrender value and is currently paying £250 a month in premiums (£3,000 a year). He believes he can achieve a 12 per cent annual return over the 12 years remaining until his mortgage is due to be repaid.

Surrender value calculation: £3,896 × 7   =£27,272
Ongoing premium calculation: £24,133 × 3   =£72,399
                                            ─────────
                                            £99,671

Peter now compares his projected total fund of £99,671 with his insurance company's projection. If it is materially more than the insurance company's figure, he should seriously consider taking over the management of his money. If there is little between the two amounts it is obviously not worth the hassle and risk of doing it himself.

Important caveats

If your initial calculations suggest that surrendering your endowment policy makes sense, there are a number of important steps to be taken:

- **Check the tax position**
  Before selling or surrendering your endowments, you should, of course, check your tax position with the Inland Revenue. For example, if you have held your policy for fewer than 10 years, or less than three quarters of the term if this is fewer than 10 years, you might be liable for higher-rate income tax on the difference between the amount you have paid into the policy and the surrender value or auction proceeds. As we have seen, this is unlikely to be very much if anything, but if you have held the policy for more than 10 years, or three quarters of the term, you are exempt so it might be worth waiting a few months if necessary.

- **Check with your mortgage lender**
  Before surrendering or selling your endowments, you should also inform your lender that you intend to do so. They will want to know how you intend to repay the mortgage, but lenders tend not to be too concerned these days as long as you convince them that you are confident of repaying your mortgage on time.

You have an obligation to keep your mortgage lender informed about material changes to the loan's backing, such as a surrender or sale of an endowment. You will need the lender's co-operation anyway, because the insurance company or auctioneer will probably ask for a letter from the bank or building society releasing their interest, if any, in the policy.

- **Maintain your life insurance**
  Before proceeding with a surrender or sale you must also make sure that your life is fully insured if necessary, because stopping the endowment will also end the life cover that comes wrapped up with the policy. If your health has deteriorated since you took out your endowment policy you may have difficulty in obtaining cover at an attractive rate. Otherwise, it is very easy to arrange a term policy to cover you for the appropriate period. Make sure there is no gap between the end of the endowment and your new cover.

  It is possible that you do not need the life cover included in your endowment policy – if you are well-covered, for example, through your job, or if you have no dependants. If you do not need life cover you will have even more to invest.

  Term insurance is a very simple product, which, as we have seen, is best treated separately rather than as part of a savings vehicle such as an endowment policy. The bad news about term insurance is that you will personally never see any benefit from the policy – either you will reach the end of the agreed term (this option is strongly recommended!) without making a claim and therefore lose all your premiums or you will die before the end of the term, in which case someone else will receive the payment. The good news, however, is that the cost of term insurance is much lower at the time of writing than it has been previously. Premiums have fallen for two main reasons. First, we are living longer so the chance of the insurance company having to pay out has reduced. Second, the market is now much more competitive, with new players such as Direct Line (tel: 0845 3000 733) and Virgin Money (tel: 08456 102040) taking on the traditional insurers and fighting for market share.

As a bare minimum you should ensure that you are covered for the full amount of your outstanding mortgage. You may also want to provide much more than this so your dependants continue to enjoy a satisfactory standard of living in the event of your death. However, that is an entirely separate matter from your mortgage-related insurance.

If, as we suggest, you choose an interest-only mortgage backed by an ISA savings scheme, you will need to select a policy which will pay the same amount throughout the term rather than the cheaper, decreasing-term type of policy which costs less because it pays out a progressively smaller amount as time passes.

The cost of term insurance varies widely so you should shop around. You should also bear in mind that you can switch between policies at any point. There is no investment element in term insurance, so if you find a cheaper deal you can simply stop paying your premiums and switch to another company. When comparing the costs of policies, you need to consider whether any change in your health might result in a higher level of premiums.

Because term insurance is so simple – and because the chance of a reasonably young person dying in the next 20 years or so is thankfully quite slim – term insurance is relatively cheap. It is, for example, much cheaper than critical illness cover where the likelihood of a payout is much greater. At the time of writing, a 30-year-old male non-smoker can buy £100,000 of cover for 25 years for as little as £7 a month, so it is an easy matter to fully cover your mortgage very cheaply.

- **Seek advice if in doubt**
  If arithmetic is not your strong point, or you have any doubts whatsoever about your endowment policy, you should obtain independent financial advice. Sofa – the Society of Financial Advisers – provides a list of 650 independent advisers who have the advanced financial planning certificate. You can find the list on the internet at www.sofa.org. Remember to ensure that the advice is truly independent and no commissions are involved. ISA mortgages are not popular in the insurance industry as they are very simple and easy to see through, so large commissions and other charges are much more visible.

THE GREATEST RISK

The suggestion that many endowment holders should consider surrendering or selling their policies will doubtless not be welcomed by most financial experts. They will say this is a dangerous course of action which puts ordinary people's savings unnecessarily at risk.

On the contrary, the greatest risk is to do nothing, letting the professionals manage your money so poorly that you find at an advanced stage in your life that you are unable to pay off the biggest debt you have ever undertaken.

Almost everyone, armed with the basic financial knowledge set out in this book, can do better for themselves, and that is why everyone with an endowment should at the least calculate whether they would be better off taking charge of their own affairs. Whether passively through tracker funds or actively through the systematic acquisition of high yielding shares, everyone has the capacity to take control of their own financial destiny.

SUMMARY

1. Many thousands of endowment policy holders are receiving letters informing them that they cannot rely on their policies to repay their mortgages as planned.
2. The past investment performance of many insurance companies has been relatively poor and their future assumptions, although set by the regulator, are worryingly low.
3. Provided you have a constructive investment plan as an alternative, it could pay to surrender many endowment policies unless they are very near maturity.
4. Everyone who has an endowment policy should at least find out how much they could raise by surrendering it. Using the insurance company's offer as a base figure plus future annual instalments they should then calculate whether they are likely to be able to outperform the insurance company by investing on their own. *On past performance* of the market as a whole, and high yielding shares in particular, 15 per cent per annum is a reasonable yardstick to use. However, to be conservative, use 12 per cent just to see if the hassle of surrendering your policies is likely to make good sense.
5. Consider auctioning or selling your endowment policy rather than surrendering it. This can raise up to 15 per cent more.

6. If your intial calculations indicate that it will pay to surrender your policy, before proceeding further it is vitally important to:

a) Keep your lender fully informed of any changes you intend to make.

b) Make sure your life is fully insured throughout, assuming that the lender insists and/or you wish to make provision for your dependants. If your health has deteriorated since you took out the endowment policy, it might be difficult to reinsure at an attractive rate.

c) Check the tax implications of surrendering to make sure that the amount you receive is tax-free and that your and your spouse's ISA allowances will be sufficient to shelter your future stock market capital gains from taxation.

d) If arithmetic is not your strong point or you are in any doubt at all about surrendering your policy, consult an *independent* financial adviser.

6

SAVE REGULARLY

*'Money is the seed of money, and the first guinea is
sometimes more difficult to acquire than the second
million.'*

Jean Jacques Rousseau

**The second part of your bid to become a millionaire depends
on shares continuing to be an outstanding financial asset. The
stock market trend has been relentlessly upwards for many
decades, with occasional short-term downward blips.
Investing regularly will help smooth out the inevitable ups
and downs. The key is to climb aboard – now.**

You are now halfway through your blueprint for financial
freedom. So far you have learned to wonder at the
miraculous power of compounding and fear its alter ego,
the inflationary dragon. You have also invested in the first
great financial asset, property, by buying your own house
or flat.

Next, you have chosen to finance the purchase of your
home in the most sensible way by avoiding a costly
endowment. Instead you will use ISAs to build a tax-free
fund with which to pay off your mortgage. If you found
yourself saddled with an endowment mortgage, you will
have calculated the pros and cons of surrendering or
selling your policy.

Now you are ready to embark on the second crucial
element of your bid to become a millionaire and achieve

financial security for you and your family. You are ready to become a stock market investor.

You can set up an ISA to protect your stock market investments from the savage attacks of income and capital gains tax. You can also benefit from the stock market in a relatively risk-free way through tracker unit trusts.

This book will show you how to become an active stock market investor, first in a cautious, formulaic way by investing in high-yield shares using a simple, easy-to-apply method. Finally, it will guide you into more active investment to help you outperform the averages and become truly wealthy.

QUELLING YOUR FEARS

First, however, we need to allay some understandable fears about the stock market. If you are to achieve your goals, you must be confident that the stock market is not a dangerous casino in which you might lose all of your hard-earned savings.

After a long period of very good returns, stock markets have performed badly over the last two years so you might be wondering if the long-term rising trend has come to a sticky end. Unit trust advertisements include the familiar warning that 'shares can go down as well as up' and there is no doubt that many new investors will begin their investment careers at a new peak for the market. Others will be more fortunate and make their first investments at the low for the year.

The key point is that *no-one* knows whether the market is going to rise or fall. If, during market hours, you could get hold of a copy of tomorrow's newspaper you could make a fortune today. Even Warren Buffett, the world's most successful investor, often says that he does not have the faintest idea of the market's direction from year to year. All he tries to do is to look for value and buy relatively well.

THE TREND IS YOUR FRIEND

The second key point, based on past performance and logic, is that the long-term trend is upward. If you want to be a millionaire you have to grit your teeth and climb aboard the stock market at some point – in our view the sooner the better.

No-one can forecast the future direction of the stock market but history shows that shares rise much more often than they fall. Look at the table overleaf, which shows the percentage rise in the stock market each year since 1962. As you can see, the market has risen in 28 years out of the last 40. Of the 12 years in which the market fell, in only six was the decline more than 10 per cent. Of the 28 rising years, 22 showed increases of more than 10 per cent and in 13 years the rise was more than 20 per cent.

A further indication of the relentless rise of the stock market is shown by the chart on page 91 of the market since 1899. Notice how the legendary crashes of 1929 and 1987, and even the savage bear market of 1973/4 and the downturn of the past couple of years, are in retrospect almost imperceptible blips, hardly registering against the steady upward trend.

BULL AND BEAR MARKETS

Despite these reassuring statistics, however, it obviously makes sense to be cautious if the market is in a particularly

Barclays Equity Index 1962–2001

Year	Index	% Change	Year	Index	% Change
1962	391	−3.0	1982	1,579	22.1
1963	450	15.2	1983	1,944	23.1
1964	405	−10.0	1984	2,450	26.0
1965	428	5.9	1985	2,822	15.2
1966	389	−9.3	1986	3,452	22.3
1967	500	28.7	1987	3,596	4.2
1968	718	43.5	1988	3,829	6.5
1969	609	−15.2	1989	4,978	30.0
1970	563	−7.5	1990	4,265	−14.3
1971	799	41.9	1991	4,907	15.1
1972	901	12.8	1992	5,635	14.8
1973	619	−31.4	1993	6,951	23.3
1974	276	−55.3	1994	6,286	−9.6
1975	653	136.3	1995	7,450	18.5
1976	628	−3.9	1996	8,320	11.7
1977	886	41.2	1997	9,962	19.7
1978	910	2.7	1998	11,048	10.9
1979	949	4.3	1999	13,396	21.2
1980	1,206	27.1	2000	12,329	−8.0
1981	1,294	7.2	2001	10,428	−15.4

Index: 1899 = 100

Source: Barclays Capital

frothy phase or there are indications that shares are likely to perform badly in coming months.

There are a number of well-known factors that traditionally point to the market's future direction. We could, for example, advise you to watch the trend of interest rates. Usually if they are rising it is bad news for markets. Another bearish sign is a bullish consensus view among investment advisers – if they are all confident that the market will go up it means that their money is already in the market so it is time to hoard a little more cash.

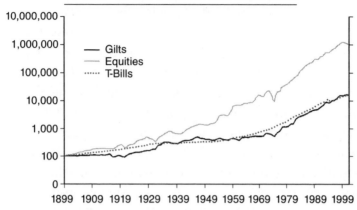

Barclays Total Return Indices: Nominal Terms, Gross Income Reinvested

Source: Barclays Capital

The number and calibre of new share issues is another signal – when they become legion and of very poor quality it is an obvious sign that there is too much money about. Perhaps the best one-liner on the market's direction is to try to determine if the mood of the market is, as the Americans say, 'cash is trash' or 'cash is king'. At the top of bull markets no-one wants to hold cash so institutional cash holdings tend to be very low. Conversely, at the bottom of bear markets cash becomes very desirable and everyone accumulates as much as possible, so a relatively small change in mood can often be greeted by a very substantial uplift in share prices as institutional and private investors rush to reinvest.

POUND/COST AVERAGING

If you are investing in tracker funds through unit trusts, there is a very simple answer to this problem that will save you having to worry about which way the market is heading. All the leading fund management groups offer investors in their unit trusts the facility to invest through savings schemes. Instead of having to invest all of your spare cash in one hit each year, you can spread your investment over the year in monthly tranches. In this way, if your first few instalments are at just the wrong time, your subsequent tranches will be invested at much more attractive prices. Say, for example, the FTSE 100 index stands at 6,000 when you begin and then drops to 5,500 one month later before drifting down to 5,000 for a few months and then rallying a few months later. This is not bad news for you because only one instalment is invested at the temporary top of 6,000, another at 5,500 and the rest at the market low. Of course, there is always the possibility that the market might not rally in your first year and the index might, for example, drift down further to 4,500 for a while. In this event, a lot of your hard-earned money will be invested at this new low and you will benefit all the more from the eventual rally.

SELF-SELECT INVESTORS

For investors who do their own thing with self-administered ISAs, phasing entry to the market is not so easy. The funds you invest as an individual will probably be insufficient to split down into monthly instalments without broker's commissions becoming far too expensive. Say you plan to invest £1,000 in a particular stock, split into twelve monthly instalments this would be just over £80 a month and the broker's minimum commission of, say, £15 would be devastating.

There is, therefore, no alternative with most self-administered funds other than to invest yearly. This does, of course, mean that you could hit the high for the year, but over the years, provided you keep investing regularly, the averages should still work out in a very similar way to a monthly investment plan. An important and very reassuring statistic from the Barclays study is that over the past 100 years, shares have outperformed gilts over a 10-year period 86 per cent of the time. The odds are firmly stacked in favour of equities.

It is very important to keep investing regularly and not be too upset by a poor first year or even second year's perform-ance. Remember that if the outlook appears very bleak to you it is looking like that to every other investor as well and share prices are usually reflecting the mood and discounting most of the bad news ahead. The best minds in the investment business cannot forecast which way the market is going, so why should you even try? Forecasting the market is an absolute waste of time, so stick to your programme and invest regularly whatever the current mood. We can confi-dently predict that some of the investments you make when the market outlook appears at its bleakest will be far more successful that those when the market looks very buoyant.

SUMMARY

1. No-one knows whether the market will rise or fall in the short term. However, history shows that the stock market rises much more often than it falls. Corrections, which at the time seem terrifying, become almost imperceptible blips in the long run.

2. A number of indicators of bull and bear markets recur and can provide a guide to the future direction of the market but timing is very difficult. You should, therefore, save in regular instalments to iron out market swings.

7

PAY LESS TAX

*'The only thing that hurts more than having to pay an
income tax is not having to pay an income tax.'*

Thomas Dewar

**ISAs, like their predecessors PEPs, are very good news for
private investors. They help you to secure your financial
freedom without worrying about tax and they help to enhance
massively the long-term value of your savings. Using ISAs to
protect your investments from income and capital gains taxes
is an essential element of your bid to become a millionaire.**

We are now assuming that you have bought your house or
flat and have wisely decided to repay your interest-only
mortgage with the proceeds of a stock market-based
savings plan. If you were already saddled with an
endowment policy, you have used the tables in Chapters 4
and 5 to calculate whether or not it makes sense to invest
your own funds and, after taking suitable advice, have
possibly surrendered or sold the policy. In this case you
will have a lump sum to kick-start your investments, but
either way you are in a position to pay a regular amount
into a savings plan. Sensibly invested this plan should pay
off your mortgage with ease and leave you with a
substantial surplus.

The next step is to consider how to invest your money
in the most flexible and tax-efficient way. You might think
tax worries are the preserve of a small minority of wealthy

people but, as you will see, a little planning now can transform your finances for the long term.

If you do not shelter your savings from tax at the outset, you will not be able to do it later. You *must* get the tax structure of your savings in place as quickly as possible, and there is no simpler or more efficient way of doing this than by setting up an Individual Savings Account (ISA).

ISAs first became available in April 1999. Strictly speaking, they are guaranteed to last for only 10 years, until 2009. However, ISAs are a tax shelter that replaced PEPs, launched in 1987, and Tax-Exempt Special Savings Accounts (Tessas), launched in 1991. It seems highly likely that ISAs, or something similar, will continue to be available beyond 2009. Our advice is based on the assumption that ISAs or an equivalent will continue indefinitely.

WHO SHOULD USE ISAs?

It is often said that ISAs are of use only to higher-rate taxpayers and those whose annual capital gains exceed the annual exemption (£7,700 in 2002/03). There is some truth in this and it is undoubtedly the case that unless you intend to save at least £2,500 a year it will be many years before you see any real benefit from your tax-free status. In the short term, it could actually cost you more in charges than you gain through lower tax payments.

However, for anyone with serious financial ambitions who is planning to save hard for an extended period of time, the benefits are likely to massively exceed the charges in future years. If you plan to become a millionaire, you should use ISAs to the maximum extent possible.

The attractions of ISAs are undoubtedly greater for higher-rate taxpayers because the charges incurred are

likely to be less than the amount they will save in income
tax from the *outset*.

For example, a higher-rate taxpayer with an unsheltered
£5,000 of shares earning a 4 per cent net dividend yield,
will receive an annual dividend of £200 on which he will
be obliged to pay an extra £50 in tax when he fills in his
tax return (because under current legislation he is liable to
pay tax at 32.5 per cent of the 'gross' dividend). This £50
is in addition to the £22.22 he is deemed to have already
paid when he received his 'net' dividend.

If he shelters his £5,000 of shares in an ISA, however, not
only will he have no further tax to pay but, until 2004, his
dividend will be enhanced by a 10 per cent tax reclaim
which will boost his dividend income by £22 to £222. In
other words, he will be £72 better off and this saving will
almost certainly be greater than the annual management
charge levied by his ISA plan provider. Charles Schwab, for
example, charges 0.75 per cent + VAT a year with a £23.50
minimum and a £141 maximum (including VAT). The
charge on a £5,000 plan would be £44.

This might sound a marginal saving, but the key point is
that in subsequent years, as the portfolio rises in value, the
income tax saving will continue to grow while the plan's
charges will rise no higher than the maximum annual rate.
Because Schwab allows you to roll subsequent years' plans
into the first, with only one management charge applicable
to the combined funds, anyone contributing the annual
ISA allowance of £7,000 a year will soon be saving a great
deal more in income tax than he is paying as a
management charge.

For a basic-rate taxpayer, the benefits of an ISA are in
the *short term* more marginal. Because basic-rate taxpayers
are deemed to have already met their tax liability on their
dividends when they were paid out 'net' of tax, the benefit

is restricted to the 10 per cent tax reclaim and the exemption from capital gains tax. As we have seen, on a £5,000 fund, earning a 4 per cent dividend yield, the income tax benefit is worth only £22 a year, which could easily be less than the management fee. In the early years, also, it is unlikely that capital gains will exceed the annual exemption.

For anyone with ambitions to become a millionaire, the key point to realise is that in the early years you may not gain much benefit from the tax-free status of your ISAs – it may even cost you a few pounds a year – but you will be building up a tax-free fund which in future years will benefit you greatly.

Even if you are not currently paying tax at the higher marginal rate, you probably have ambitions to earn more than the £34,500 a year beyond which your marginal income is taxed at 40 per cent. When you move into this higher tax band you will not need to worry at all about an increased tax liability on your shares if you have sheltered them in ISAs.

Moreover, because of the wonderful power of compounding, you will hope to soon amass a portfolio on which, unsheltered by an ISA, you will start to be liable for capital gains tax. If you increase the value of your shares at 15 per cent a year, you only need have shares worth £51,000 to exceed the annual £7,700 capital gains tax exemption. This could happen relatively quickly, especially if you are saving close to the annual £7,000 ISA limit each year.

Because the major benefit of investing in an ISA for a basic-rate taxpayer is the exemption from capital gains tax, the benefit will obviously accrue more quickly the more you save. Because of this, if you are a basic-rate taxpayer, you should wait until you have close to the annual £7,000 limit before opening an ISA. If you are a higher-rate taxpayer it is worth your while to do so at a lower level, but even for someone paying 40 per cent tax it is not worth opening an ISA with less than about £2,500.

These guideline figures are based on the sort of charges levied by Charles Schwab. When deciding on the best ISA, look for a similar sort of charging structure. In particular, choose an ISA that sets a maximum cash charge. Avoid those that charge a percentage fee irrespective of the value of your holdings. Bear in mind, too, that you need to take account of dealing charges and the number of different shares you want to invest in to spread your risk. Even a direct investment in shares of £2,500 would not make much sense unless you intended to invest the same amount each year over a number of years to build up a portfolio that spreads the risk.

Two other points on charges, especially relevant to basic-rate taxpayers. Many small investors have put tiny parcels of privatisation or windfall shares in an ISA. Year after year, charges outweigh any tax credit reclaimed and these investors may never face a capital gains tax bill even if they hold the shares outside an ISA. They may, therefore, be wasting their money by holding their shares in an ISA.

However, for the serious small investor who intends to build up a substantial portfolio over many years, saving capital gains tax through an ISA becomes more of an issue. Also, at some stage, perhaps in retirement, long-term investments will be turned into income to spend. At this point, you may want to convert shares into higher-yielding gilts or corporate bonds. Then, the income tax saving afforded by ISAs will become much more relevant.

Secondly, specific ISA charges usually apply only to 'self-select' ISAs, where you invest directly in shares you choose yourself. Most unit trust-based ISAs levy no extra ISA charges. You pay only those charges you would pay anyway even if you invested in the unit trust outside an ISA. In this case, the question of whether ISA charges outweigh any tax saving does not arise – so you might as well invest through an ISA. The most important point to bear in mind when weighing up whether or not an ISA is worthwhile for you is that *you cannot use past years' ISA allowances*. If you build up a sizeable fund outside the shelter of an ISA and then find yourself paying capital gains or extra income tax on your shares, you will only be able to shelter your fund at a maximum rate of £7,000 a year going forward. You may find yourself in a position where it will take you several years simply to shelter your *existing* funds let alone your continuing savings.

THE POWER OF COMPOUNDING AGAIN

To understand why ISAs are such a godsend to serious investors, especially higher-rate taxpayers, let us return to the miracle of compounding. Imagine a 30-year-old married man, Donald, who has just read *How to Become a Millionaire* and decides to invest the maximum allowance for himself and his wife in a tracker-fund ISA each year for the next 20 years. He, therefore, opens two ISAs for £7,000, one for himself and one for his wife.

Over the next nine years Donald will contribute a further £63,000 into his ISA and £63,000 into his wife's, for a total of £140,000. Now imagine that during this period the stock market grows at an average overall return of 12 per cent a year and that this is fully reflected in the performance of his tracker funds. By the end of the 20-year period, the two ISAs are transformed by this relatively undemanding annual return into a total fund worth £1.1m, *which has the enormous advantage of being completely tax-free.*

An individual's ISA allowance expires on 5 April each year. If you have not taken advantage of it, you will not be able to go back later. The benefit will have gone and you will pay a heavy price for the omission in future years.

WHAT EXACTLY IS AN ISA?

We have mentioned in passing the annual allowance for contributing to an ISA. At this point, we should explain the key features of ISAs and the rules that govern them. An ISA is nothing more than a tax-efficient pot in which you may keep and grow your savings, whether they be in the form of cash, shares or even life assurance.

There are limits on the kind of investments you can shelter in an ISA. For example, you cannot buy shares quoted on the Alternative Investment Market but you can hold shares quoted on a recognised overseas exchange. Unlike with PEPs, there are no global invest-ment restrictions so you could, if you choose, hold all your investments in a fund investing in non UK or European shares. You are also allowed to hold gilts with more than five years to run to maturity and you can hold bank or building society deposits and money market unit trusts.

ISAs are available to anyone who is aged 18 or over and resident for tax purposes in the UK. You are generally considered resident if you are in the UK for more than half a year for several years in succession. If you are using your ISAs to finance the purchase of your home, this is obviously likely to be the case.

Each person has an annual allowance of £7,000. This means that a man and his wife can, between them, shelter £14,000 a year in ISAs.

An ISA can have up to three component parts: life assurance, cash and stocks and shares. Of the £7,000 limit, no more than £3,000 can be in cash and no more than £1,000 in the form of a life insurance product.

As already explained, confusing life insurance with savings is inadvisable, so obviously it is not recommended that you should even consider putting this kind of product into your ISA. As it is possible to generate a much better return from the stock market than can be achieved from a deposit account, you should also not give a second thought to using your ISA limit for cash savings. The full amount can, and should, be used for shares.

The beauty of an ISA is that once you have set it up you can for all practical purposes forget about tax on the shares held within it. You will not be liable for income tax on the dividends paid by the companies in which you hold shares. In fact until 2004 you will also benefit from the repayment to you of a notional 10 per cent tax charge that is deemed to have been paid by the company to the Exchequer before the 'net' dividend was paid to you by the company. This means that if a company declares a 9p dividend, your ISA manager will reclaim 1p from the taxman and add it to your account.

Where capital gains tax is concerned, you can forget about it completely. The taxman does not even need to know how much your ISAs are worth. As far as your annual tax return is concerned, these savings do not exist.

FUND-BASED ISAs

There are two main types of ISA and they tend to charge in different ways. If you decide you want someone else to make all the investment decisions, we recommend you use your annual ISA allowance to buy a tracker fund. These kinds of funds tend to charge a small annual percentage fee related to the size of your investment. If you decide to opt for a tracker fund you do not really need to worry any more about the ISA aspect of it. It simply comes as part of the package and competition in the market means that charges are very similar between providers. A typical example is Virgin's Maxi ISA – Investing for Growth, which charges a 1 per cent annual management fee, calculated and deducted daily from your fund. There is no initial fee and no other charges apply. You can invest as little as £1 as a lump sum or £1 a month. The fund aims to track the performance of the FT-A All Share index. We explain in more detail how to invest in a tracker fund in the next chapter.

SELF-SELECT ISAs

The second type of ISA is the self-select variety, in which you choose your own investments and the ISA provider simply administers your fund, reclaiming your dividend credits and holding your share certificates for you in a nominee account. In Chapters 9, 10 and 11 we show you a variety of ways to select the shares for your self-select ISA.

A self-select ISA is potentially more complex and could cost you more in charges than a tracker fund if you are not careful. A good first port of call is the Moneyextra website (www.moneyextra.co.uk) which has a section explaining all the ins and outs of ISAs, with links to ISA providers and a wealth of explanatory information.

Most self-select ISAs are provided by stockbrokers. These include traditional brokers such as Killik & Co, which have offices around the country. The telephone and internet-based execution-only companies such as Charles Schwab and The Share Centre are also heavily involved. Finally, the stockbroking arms of high street banks such as Barclays and Halifax offer self-select ISAs.

For a comprehensive list of ISA providers take a look at the Moneyextra website.

WHAT TO LOOK FOR

There are three main considerations when choosing a self-select ISA provider:

1. What restrictions, if any, will apply to the investments you can buy?
2. What are the charges?
3. How efficient is the provider's administration?

Restrictions

Self-selection means exactly what it says – you can choose the investments to put in your ISA wrapper. In practice, however, not many providers will give you a full choice at a sensible price. For example, ISA rules allow you to invest in shares listed on recognised non-UK stock exchanges. However, some providers will charge you a higher rate of commission to deal in overseas shares. Killik & Co, for example, charges 1.65 per cent for the first £15,000 in UK shares, with a minimum of £40 but 2.5 per cent on the first £10,000 of overseas shares with a £75 minimum. If you are likely to invest only in UK shares, which is to be recommended for all but the most experienced investors, this will obviously not be a concern.

Charges

Self-select ISAs do not usually charge initial fees, but have an annual management charge. This is usually expressed as a percentage of the value of your investments, sometimes with a minimum and/or maximum. It has already been shown that the value of your ISA can rise substantially over the years, so always go for a provider which quotes a maximum annual charge. Very soon it should become insignificant in relation to the size of your fund.

The next charge to look at closely is the cost of buying and selling shares. The cost of dealing will normally be expressed as a percentage of the size of deal, with a minimum charge of between £2.50 and £15, sometimes with a maximum. Again look favourably on a provider which is prepared to cap its dealing charge for larger deals. This could save you a considerable sum in later years.

Here are a couple of examples of charges which were in force at the time of writing:

Halifax – a flat dealing rate of £12.50 for up to £2,500, £22.50 up to £60,000 (over £60,000 is negotiable), no initial fee but an annual charge of 0.6 per cent + VAT with a £30.55 minimum and a £117.50 maximum (including VAT). There are no additional charges for dividend and tax credit collection.

Charles Schwab – an execution-only broker – has no initial fee for its ISAs but an annual charge of 0.75 per cent + VAT, with a yearly minimum of £23.50 and a maximum of £141. Dealing costs range from £12 to a maximum of £75, depending on whether you deal by touchtone, internet or over the telephone. The Schwab self-select ISA appears very attractive to long-term investors with substantial financial ambitions, because the charges, both annual and for dealing, have very low ceilings. By the time your fund has grown to £100,000 or so the charges will be almost immaterial.

Efficiency

Finally, you must look at the relative efficiency or otherwise of the ISA provider. There is no point in having the cheapest deal if you cannot get through on the phone or via the internet to place an order. This is especially true when the market is moving fast and some of the quicker-growing execution-only brokers have been criticised for their level of service on particularly active trading days.

ISAs VERSUS PENSIONS REVISITED

In Chapter 4 on financing your home, we pointed out that the choice between using an ISA or a pension to finance the repayment of your mortgage is a fine one. The reason for this is that pensions enjoy a massive advantage because their immunity to tax is enjoyed up-front. For every £78 an employee pays into a personal pension, the plan provider claims back basic-rate tax of £22. In addition, higher-rate taxpayers will get an extra £28 in tax relief once they have declared the contribution on their tax return. Self-employed people who pay into a personal pension plan get all their tax relief through their tax return. A gross contribution of £100 will knock £22 off a basic-rate taxpayer's tax bill and £40 off a higher-rate taxpayer's bill. The net result, whether you are employed or self-employed, is that every £100 invested in a personal plan costs a basic rate taxpayer only £78 and a higher-rate taxpayer only £60.

The power of compounding means that enjoying this money up-front can make a huge difference to the eventual value of your savings. To see how this works, imagine investing £600 a year in an ISA at 15 per cent for 20 years. The final fund in this case would be worth £70,700. Now compare this with someone investing £1,000 a year, a combination of a £600 contribution with a £400 a year tax rebate. This fund grows over the same period, and assuming the same 15 per cent rate of return, to £118,000. On the face of it, this is a much more attractive final sum, but there are some significant disadvantages in saving this way which, in our view, still tip the balance in favour of ISAs.

First, if you are using your pension to repay a mortgage you need to remember that you are allowed to take only a quarter of your final fund as a tax-free lump sum at your chosen retirement date. This means that you must achieve a fund at least four times your outstanding mortgage to ensure you can pay it off on time.

Second, although you can leave the remaining three quarters of your fund in the market when you retire, at the age of 75 you can be compelled to acquire an annuity with the money you have accumulated. If interest rates remain low, you could end up acquiring only a relatively low annual income with your retirement fund.

Third, the annuity you are compelled to buy will be taxed unlike the income from your ISA fund, which you can withdraw completely tax-free as and when you need it.

Fourth, when you, or in some circumstances your surviving spouse, die, your pension fund is kept by the insurance company from whom you have acquired the annuity. With an ISA, your savings are passed on just like the rest of your estate to your descendants.

Fifth, with no time limit, you can continue investing your ISA fund for the rest of your life, simply withdrawing as much as you choose to live on each year. If annuity rates are low you are very likely to be much better off continuing to invest your fund at, say, 12–15 per cent, withdrawing an income as you go.

It is hard to overstate the great flexibility of an ISA and, for this reason, we consider it easily the best way to invest, whether to pay off a mortgage or for any other reason.

USING YOUR CAPITAL GAINS TAX ALLOWANCE

If you are starting from scratch, and do not intend to buy a palace, you will probably find that the combined ISA allowance for you and your spouse will be more than enough to shelter all your investments, both to pay off your mortgage and to save for your retirement. However, if you plan to save more than £14,000 a year between you, or if you are starting with a lump sum as a result of surrendering an endowment policy or from an inheritance, for example, you will need to manage your investments in a way that minimises the amount of capital gains tax you become liable to pay.

There are two main ways to do this:

1. Share your investments between yourself and your spouse. This is particularly important if your spouse is not working or pays a lower rate of income tax than you.
2. Sell enough shares each year to make sure you use up your combined allowances. In 2002/03 you are allowed to make a capital gain of £7,700 each before you become liable to tax.

Capital gains tax is a complex area so you should take advice from an expert. Broadly speaking, however, gains above your annual tax-free limit attract tax at your marginal income tax rate. So, for example, if your salary puts you in the higher tax bracket any taxable capital gains you make will likewise attract the top rate of tax.

If your spouse is not working, or pays a lower rate of tax, it obviously makes sense for them to incur the capital gain rather than you. A non-taxpayer who has no income could combine the annual personal allowance of £4,615 in 2002/03 (for those under 65) and the annual capital gains tax exemption of £7,700 to make gains of £12,315 without paying tax. Above this level, too, they will pay less capital gains tax than you would until they also enter the higher rate tax band.

Ensure that enough of your shares are held in your spouse's name to allow you to manage your affairs efficiently in this way. And stay married!

PUTTING IT INTO PRACTICE

We hope we have made it clear to you that you should take up as much as you can of your annual ISA allowance. Having decided how much you wish to save, your next choice is between a managed fund ISA, which leaves the investment decisions to someone else or a self-select ISA in which you choose the shares yourself.

If you opt for a managed fund, you should go for an index tracker. The next chapter explains why trackers tend to outperform active fund managers and shows you how to choose from the many funds on offer.

If you decide to take control of share selection yourself, shop around for the best value self-select ISA on the basis of annual and dealing charges and all-round efficiency. All that remains then is the small question of which shares to buy to put in your ISA. Chapters 9, 10 and 11 will address this issue.

SUMMARY

1. ISAs, like their predecessors PEPs, are a wonderful tax perk. They allow most investors to secure their financial future without having to give much thought to tax. Not only do you avoid paying income tax on dividends or capital gains tax, you do not even have to declare your ISA shareholdings for tax purposes.
2. Thanks to the power of compounding, avoiding tax on your investments can massively increase the final value of your savings. You should ensure as many of your investments as possible are held within the tax-free wrapper of an ISA.
3. ISAs are unnecessarily complicated but you need not worry about most of the detail. Investors with serious financial ambitions should try to take up as much as possible of their annual allowances. They can invest up to £7,000 a year for both themselves and their spouses.
4. Do not worry unduly about the charges levied by ISA providers if you are saving at least £2,500 a year. If you choose a provider which caps its charges at a reasonable level, they will pale into insignificance as your fund grows in size.
5. ISAs have the edge over pensions, the other main tax-free savings vehicle. Although they do not enjoy the up-front tax advantage of a pension, they are far more flexible and under current legislation remain tax-free for the rest of your life. You can also leave your ISA

fund to your family when you die.

6. Minimise the capital gains tax you have to pay if you are saving more than £14,000 a year or are starting out with a lump sum which you cannot fully shelter from tax. Share your investments with your spouse to use up both of your allowances and sell enough shares each year to crystallise the gains you are allowed to make tax-free each year.

7. If you go for a tracker fund, the tax-free ISA wrapper usually comes with no extra charges. If you decide to go down the self-select route, choose an ISA provider using these three main criteria:

   a) What restrictions if any limit the investments you can buy for your ISA.
   b) The level of charges.
   c) The provider's administrative efficiency.

8

TRACKER FUNDS

'Money is like a sixth sense without which you cannot make a complete use of the other five.'

Somerset Maugham

Most people do not have the inclination, the expertise or sufficient time to invest directly in the stock market. They, therefore, prefer to invest in collective funds like unit trusts and open-ended investment companies. Provided you start early enough, low-cost unit trusts designed to simply track the stock market's main indices should enable you to succeed in your bid to become a millionaire.

By now, you can see clearly the need to invest in property and you understand the need to shelter your investments from tax in an ISA. However, it is more than likely that you do not have the slightest interest in actually venturing forth into the stock market to buy and sell your own shares. You might, for example, have plenty of other interests and simply cannot be bothered at the end of a busy day to devote any time to getting to grips with investment jargon.

No problem. It is quite possible to benefit from the wonderful growth of property and shares in a totally passive way, letting someone else make all the investment decisions for you. All you need to do is pay regularly into a pooled savings plan such as a unit trust and let time and compounding weave their magic.

Whole books are written on pooled investments, providing a mass of information you will probably never need to use. This chapter will be restricted to what you really need to know by concentrating on unit trusts and open-ended investment companies, because this should be more than enough to satisfy your ambition to become a millionaire. Once you understand the generalities, the focus will be on tracker funds, because they have the lowest management charges and perform better than the vast majority of actively managed unit trusts.

UNIT TRUSTS AND OPEN-ENDED INVESTMENT COMPANIES

A unit trust is a pooled investment in which thousands of small savers invest their money. You can invest as little as £20 a month or, for a lump-sum investment, £250. There is no ceiling on how much you can buy.

A newer type of fund – the Oeic – is now also available. The Oeic – open-ended investment company – works in much the same way as a unit trust from an investor's point of view, although its legal structure is different. A unit trust usually has two prices – a higher price at which investors buy and a lower price at which they can sell their units. An Oeic has a single price, but the net result to investors is much the same because there are separate charges which take into account the two prices.

Managers invest the money coming into their funds from private and institutional investors. They use it to buy shares in British and overseas companies, gilts and corporate bonds. Exactly what the managers decide to buy depends on the investment criteria of the specific trust (there is a vast range on offer) and their view of the best opportunities. With the muscle of millions of pounds under their control, they have the advantage of being able to negotiate keen prices and competitive rates of commission.

An investor has an indirect share in a fund's underlying investments, with the advantage of a portfolio spread over many different companies and sectors. Usually, the fund's investments are valued every working day and the total value of the unit trust portfolio is divided by the number of units or Oeic shares in issue. Each investor buys a number of units/shares and the value of each changes, either up or down, every time the portfolio is revalued. The value of the underlying portfolio is constantly changing and the managers will always sell units/shares or buy them back from you at any time, because they can create or cancel them to meet demand.

Unless you arrange for dividends to be reinvested, you will usually receive them from your holding twice a year, although some income funds pay out more frequently. Dividends are paid with tax already deducted. Starting rate (currently 10 per cent) and basic rate (currently 22 per cent) taxpayers have no more tax to pay. Non-taxpayers cannot reclaim this tax while higher rate taxpayers will have to pay more. As you will be holding your trusts in an ISA, however, this should not be of any further concern to you. You will also not have to pay the capital gains tax that would otherwise apply if you exceed your annual exemption limit.

CHARGES

Not surprisingly, there is a price to pay for the advantages of size and spread offered by a pooled fund. Your profits will be reduced by the charges paid to the management group to cover its fees for running the fund – initial charges when you buy and an annual fee.

Charges vary from fund to fund, but the initial fee (front-end load) is usually 5–6 per cent and is included in the bid/offer spread, which is the difference between the buying and selling price of the units. The offer price is the one you pay when you buy and the bid price the one you receive when you sell – usually about 5 or 6 per cent lower. About half of this goes as commission to your financial adviser if you use one, but you usually still pay 5 per cent even if you buy direct from the company.

Because of the bid/offer spread, if you bought units in the morning and sold them in the afternoon, you would receive 5 per cent less than you paid. In other words, before you can start to make profits, the units must rise by more than 5 per cent. The same applies to Oeics, because there are charges alongside the single buying and selling price. It is a costly process dealing in and out of these funds, so bear this in mind. For example, if you bought units when the bid (selling) and offer (buying) prices were 100p and 106p, and sold when they were 127p and 133p, you would buy at 106p and sell at 127p. Your gain would, therefore, be only 21p (127p minus 106p). *The performance figures of unit trusts allow for the spread between the bid and offer prices, which is one of the reasons that unit trusts do not, on average, keep level with the market as a whole.* Annual charges range between 0.3 and 2 per cent and these are deducted from dividends, or from the capital, before they are paid out to you.

SAFETY

There are two types of risk you face when buying unit trusts and Oeics. One is that someone will run off with your money and the other that the value of your investment will fall. Only the second is a real possibility.

Unit trusts and Oeics are tightly controlled by law and all managers must be registered with the Financial Services Authority. In the very unlikely event that the fund manager or an adviser were to steal some money from the trust, a compensation scheme would pay out a maximum of £48,000 to each unit holder. This is made up of 100 per cent of the first £30,000 and 90 per cent of the next £20,000 of an individual's investment. You cannot claim compensation if your investment simply loses value because of indifferent management or a fall in the market as a whole. However, as your money is spread over a vast range of different companies, there is less chance of a catastrophe than if you had bought individual shares.

Several management groups run a share exchange scheme, which enables you to swap any existing shares you own into their fund. Some will give you a better deal than if you had sold the shares on the market yourself. Others simply sell your shares for you and charge the appropriate commission. A generous exchange scheme can be a cost-effective way of disposing of small parcels of shares, particularly from privatisation issues.

SHOULD YOU BUY UNIT TRUSTS AND OEICS?

There are three good reasons why so many people invest in pooled funds instead of investing in shares directly:

1. An individual may not have enough money to invest in a sufficiently wide spread of shares to reduce the risk to an acceptable level. However attractive an individual share may appear to be, there is always the danger that

something totally unexpected might happen that could cripple the company in question. For example, a leading company in the drugs industry might discover that some of its drugs had unfortunate side-effects and, as a result, could be sued by the patients who had suffered. If all of your money was invested in companies like these, you could suffer sudden and sickening losses. However expert you are at investment, you need to spread your risk. A unit trust or Oeic invests in a large number of shares and will achieve this important objective for you.

2. The cost of buying and selling shares in very small amounts is excessive. For a transaction involving only £100 worth of stock, for example, you could find yourself paying a high minimum charge with a total cost of as much as 25 per cent or more of your investment. It is only when you begin to deal in sums of about £1,000 per share that charges fall to 1.5–4 per cent and become at all reasonable.

3. Most funds require a minimum investment of £500 but some allow investments of £250 and, with a regular savings plan, you can invest as little as £20 a month. It is not economic to invest such small amounts in the stock market directly.

It would be good to be able to add a fourth reason for buying pooled funds – the advantage of obtaining professional management of your portfolio. Unfortunately unit trust managers have in general failed to beat the market.

Standard & Poor's provides performance figures for 1,106 unit trusts or Oeics with a five-year record to the end of March 2002.

The figures can be compared with the performance of a number of benchmarks. One useful benchmark is the FT-

A All Share index. Of those 1,106 funds, only 315 beat the
FT-A All Share index. To put that another way, over 70 per
cent of the funds failed to beat this index.

It is fair to argue that not all the funds would have tried
or expected to beat the market. For example, cash and
bond-based funds are lower risk investments that you
would not expect to compare well with share-based funds.
It may also be fair to argue that it is wrong to compare
funds investing in Japan or Emerging markets with the FT-
A All Share index, which measures UK companies. The
success or otherwise of those funds should be compared
with other more relevant indices. However, when you
invest in shares you want the best returns. There is little
consolation in investing in the best-performing Japanese
fund if Japan is the wrong sector to be in over the period
of your investment.

Narrowing the analysis does not make for better
reading. Of 211 funds in the UK companies sector, only 45
beat the FT-A All Share index over five years. So, nearly 80
per cent underperformed the market. The UK Smaller
Companies sector did rather better. Of 64 funds, 21
outperformed the benchmark. This is a 'failure' rate of only
67 per cent. UK Equity Income funds were the best of the
bunch with 37 out of 78 funds beating the market average,
but this is still less than half the total.

Standard & Poor's has prepared the unit trust
performance statistics on an offer-to-bid basis which is the
accepted measure, albeit a harsh one, because it deducts
all charges. If you were to buy shares directly in the stock
market there would also be some charges, so the
comparison is not a totally fair one. However, the fact
remains that most actively managed funds underperform
the market.

TRACKER FUNDS

There is a simple way of beating the performance of most pooled funds – buy a tracker fund. Trackers are unit trusts that do no more than try to mirror the performance of a share index. Tracker fund managers may use different techniques but, typically, they will buy all the shares in an index in exact proportion to the weighting of each share in the index they are tracking. For example, if the shares of one company represent 5 per cent of the market value of all the companies covered by the index, then 5 per cent of the value of the shares bought will be that company's shares. When new money comes into the fund, shares will be bought in the correct proportion. Likewise, shares will be sold in the correct proportions should there be a net outflow of investors' funds. Apart from dealing to accommodate the inflows and outflows of investors' money, the only other time tracker fund managers have to trade is when shares are removed from the index and replaced by new constituents. This means they save costs by not switching their investments too frequently.

Tracker funds never match the performance of their chosen index exactly; they have some expenses to pay, they do not always hold every share in the index and sometimes the funds have to sell shares to refund outgoing investors. But the time spent on management by the tracker funds is relatively minuscule, so their charges are very much less than other fund managers. For example, Gartmore's UK Index Fund, which tracks the FT-A All-Share Index, *has no initial charge and just an average 0.5 per cent spread between the buying and selling prices.* This is a tremendous advantage that saves investors from starting with a 5–6 per cent handicap. In addition, the Gartmore tracker fund's annual charge is only 0.5 per cent a year or 1 per cent if you invest through an ISA.

Index-tracking funds have acquired popularity in recent years, with the result that an increasing number of fund managers have launched tracker funds. Standard & Poor's has performance figures for only 12 funds tracking the FT-A All Share index over the five years to the end of March 2002. The All Share index would have turned £1,000 into £1,386, assuming that net income was reinvested. Top tracker Fidelity Moneybuilder turned £1,000 into £1,394, roughly in line with the index. Deutsche UK Equity Index Tracker was bottom of the 12 funds. It turned £1,000 into £1,234, a shortfall of 11 per cent. However, that still compares favourably with most actively managed funds.

Eleven funds tracked the FTSE 100 index over the same five years. The FTSE 100 would have turned £1,000 into £1,385 assuming net income was reinvested. The top performer was Scottish Widows UK Index, which had turned £1,000 into £1,351, again assuming net income was reinvested. The Scottish Widows fund fell short of matching the market by 2.5 per cent. Sovereign FTSE 100 fund came eleventh out of the eleven, turning £1,000 into £1,214, a shortfall of 12 per cent compared with the index. That is a large shortfall, but certainly no worse than the performance of many actively managed funds.

Two possible problems with FTSE 100 trackers have emerged recently. One is the increasing domination of the FTSE 100 index by a handful of giant multi-national corporations. Vodafone, for example, was worth around 14 per cent of the whole FTSE 100 index at its peak. Strict rules governing unit trusts restrict investment in one company to 10 per cent of the value of the total portfolio. This makes life a bit more difficult for managers to track the index. It also means that a few large companies form a disproportionate part of the value of the FTSE 100. If the share price of one of these mega-companies falls out of favour – as Vodafone's has in the fallout from the 1999–2000 tech boom – it will have an adverse effect on the performance of a fund tracking the index.

The second problem is related to the rise and fall of Vodafone. During the tech boom, some of the new, high-tech dot.com companies were valued out of all proportion to their turnover or profits. In fact many had not made profits at all and were not expected to do so for several years, if ever. But their inflated market capitalisations propelled them into the FTSE 100, pushing out of the index a number of well-established, profitable companies. This was a relatively short-lived phenomenon, but funds that tracked the index were obliged to buy shares in the new companies and sell those in the old companies which have fallen out of the index. This undoubtedly made funds that tracked the FTSE 100 more risky and volatile. This is not an argument against investing in these funds, but a warning to investors of a possible downside they must appreciate. Funds that track the FT-A All Share should be a little less volatile.

SURVIVAL OF THE FITTEST

It may seem to be a modest objective simply to match the market. However, as you can see from the lamentable performance of many actively managed unit trusts and Oeics, keeping up with the indices is far easier said than done. One of the reasons for this is the high initial charges you pay when you subscribe for a conventional fund. The other is the way the indices are computed. Companies that fail to make the grade and shrink in size are automatically kicked out by the stock market's Review Panel, which meets once a quarter to review and decide upon the constituents. Its main criterion for selection is size as measured by stock market value, so most new entrants tend to be expanding companies. There is, therefore, a kind of automatic Darwin-like process which chops out companies that have faltered and replaces them with more vigorous ones. In addition, when changes are made, there is no deduction for commission or stamp duty. This means that fund managers are competing against excellent portfolio management operating without cost.

Research, conducted by the *Observer* newspaper, showed that in 1993 the FTSE 100 Index, the market's most popular measure, was 500 points higher than it would have been had it stuck with its original constituents (the index was first compiled in 1984). In other words, 25 per cent of the index's 2,000 point rise since it started life at a base figure of 1,000 had been achieved by switching into companies as they entered the index and selling shares in those companies that were demoted. If you think about it, the outperformance is very logical and is another compelling argument in favour of tracker funds.

TWO KEY BONUSES

It appears from the evidence of past performance, that Fidelity Moneybuilder, Hill Samuel UK Equity, Legal & General UK Index, Dresdner RCM UK Index and Gartmore's UK Index offer the best choice of funds that track the FT-A All Share index. All of these fund management groups also offer two additional services.

1. They will set up and administer ISAs for you to shelter your future capital profits and to have the 10 per cent

tax credit on share dividends reclaimed until April 2004 (when this concession ends). They may charge you for this service but the costs are relatively negligible compared with the benefit of paying no taxation. For example, there is an extra 0.5 per cent + VAT per annum charge on Gartmore's UK Index ISA.

2. They will help you to invest through a regular savings plan. Instead of investing a lump sum annually you can, for example, invest monthly. As we saw in Chapter 6, this is another great boon to private investors as it enables them to spread the risk of investing all of their funds in the market at just the wrong time. Provided you keep investing regularly you will smooth out market swings. Some of your instalments will be near a temporary market top but others will be right at the bottom. The averages are on your side and you should eventually benefit from the long-term upward trend.

Fortunately, you do not have to do much work yourself in setting up the ISAs and savings plans. You simply need to fill in the appropriate forms with the fund management groups that you have chosen to manage your trackers.

WHY TRACKERS ARE A GOOD THING

The authors are active stock market investors and take the view that the application of skill and experience can result in *consistent* outperformance of the market. Nearly matching the market over an extended period should be more than enough to make you relatively wealthy. To satisfy the stated goal of this book – to help you become a millionaire and achieve financial freedom for yourself and your family, however, you will probably need to go one step further and learn the basics of active investment.

The stock market tends to rise much more often than it falls and the average rise, compounded year after year, is almost guaranteed to make you very wealthy *if you start early enough and save regularly.*

In the next three chapters, we will show you ways in which we believe you can outperform the market and, therefore, accelerate the achievement of your financial goals.

SUMMARY

1. Not everyone wants to be an active investor and letting someone else make your investment decisions for you should not hold you back in your bid to become a millionaire.
2. Pooled investments offer some substantial advantages. They provide the security of a wide spread of shares and allow small amounts to be invested regularly at a reasonable cost.
3. Tracker funds are the best kinds of collective investment. By definition, they match the performance of the market, which most funds do not. They also have lower costs because they are easier to manage and deal less frequently than active funds.
4. Setting up a tracker fund ISA is very simple and investing in the stock market in this way allows you to get on with your life without any further hassle.

9

HIGH YIELDERS

*'It is better to have a permanent income than to be
fascinating.'*

Oscar Wilde

**Investing in the stock market through tracker funds will more
than likely make you very wealthy if you start early enough
and invest regularly. However, a cautious approach like this
means you will never benefit fully from the exciting share
price rises that are the goal of more active investors. Simply
paying into a tracker fund ISA is rather dull for people with
real financial ambitions. As a first step for investors who
want a half-way house between pooled funds and active stock
market investment, a systematic approach to buying solid
blue-chip shares is advisable. It is very simple, requires
little knowledge of investment and has consistently outperformed the market over extended periods.**

As we saw in the last chapter, investing in the stock market
through a tracker fund is a cost-effective and simple way
of gaining exposure to the wonderful long-term growth of
shares.

As proved earlier, however, even a small outperformance each year can, thanks to the magical power of
compounding, result in a massive enhancement of your
eventual wealth. For this reason, many investors, ourselves
included, strive to beat the market each year.

If you are not an expert, achieving this goal might seem an impossible task. However, we believe that even novice investors can beat the market consistently by applying a tried and tested investment approach, which focuses on buying high-yield shares. The method is likely to appeal to less experienced investors because it also invests exclusively in leading blue-chip shares with familiar household names.

This chapter explains why the technique works and shows you in a step-by-step way how it is put into practice. If you want to go one step beyond passive tracker fund investment but do not feel sufficiently confident to try full-blown active stock market investment, this is the strategy for you.

TANGIBLE APPROACH

Earnings growth, undervalued assets and a high dividend yield are three of the most important reasons for an investor to buy a share. A high dividend yield is certainly the most tangible of the three. Earnings and assets can be fudged by unscrupulous management but dividends, like cash, are a matter of fact.

Of the main approaches, high-yield investing is the simplest to understand and apply, especially if you are new to shares. It is possible to be a successful income investor with comparatively little effort so, if you like the idea of gaining an edge over tracker fund investors but do not wish to devote too much time to your investments, this is the method for you.

In this chapter we will show you why high-yield shares are likely to outperform the market. We will then lead you through a step-by-step method for selecting high-yielders.

You can do this as little as once a year and will need nothing more complicated or expensive to make your selections than a Sunday newspaper. The whole process should take less than an hour, but even this modest effort should enable you to significantly outperform the averages.

DIVIDEND YIELD

Before we see why and how high-yield shares have outperformed the market, we should first explain that a yield is calculated by expressing the annual dividend as a percentage of the share price. Imagine a company, Feelgood, which pays a dividend of 2.1p and has a share price of 100p. Feelgood's dividend payout of 2.1p per share, therefore, represents 2.1 per cent of the 100p share price, calculated like this:

2.1p/100p × 100 = 2.1 per cent

If the share price of Feelgood were to rise from 100p to 150p, the dividend yield would fall to 1.4 per cent (2.1p/150p × 100 = 1.4 per cent). Conversely, if Feelgood fell out of favour and its share price dropped to 50p, the yield would rise to 4.2 per cent. As a result of its fall from grace, and assuming Feelgood's directors continued to pay a dividend at the same level, the share would become, relatively speaking, a high yielder.

BEATING THE DOW

The doyen of high-yield investing is an American fund manager named Michael O'Higgins. His best-known book, *Beating the Dow*, explains his system of investing in high-yield stocks and although he tested his theory some years ago now, the basic principles of his method are as relevant today as they have ever been. It is an easy and excellent read and if you decide to make this aspect of investing your focus, you should get hold of a copy. *Beating the Dow* is available from Amazon and costs £9.39.

O'Higgins demonstrated clearly that over a long period high-yielding stocks, *with dividends reinvested*, beat the Dow Jones Industrial Average by a wide margin. Over the 18.5 years from 1973 to 1991, an investor following his basic high-yield system would have enjoyed an *average annual gain* of 16.1 per cent compared with only 10.4 per cent on the Dow. The cumulative gain before taxation over the period was 1,750 per cent for his high-yielding stocks, which means that a £1,000 investment would have grown to £18,500. This compares with only 560 per cent for the Dow average – £1,000 growing to £6,600. Two refinements to his basic system produced even better results.

The authors conducted similar research over the 15-year period from 1984 to 1998 and reached exactly the same conclusion. In the UK, too, high-yielders performed significantly better on average than the market.

THE SIZE FACTOR

O'Higgins's case for high yielders has three elements, the first of which is size. O'Higgins believes that size matters in investment and restricts his share selections to the market's largest companies. He only considers investing in the 30 American companies that constitute the Dow Jones Industrial Average, companies that are all of such a size and substance that *even in extreme circumstances* they are unlikely to fail completely.

To understand the importance of excluding a complete failure from your portfolio of shares, imagine the impact of a total loss from one stock on a small portfolio of five shares. If the value of each share was £1,000 at the outset, the total loss of one of them would at a stroke reduce the value of the portfolio from £5,000 to £4,000.

Making good this shortfall would put an enormous strain on the other shares. They would have to rise by an average of 25 per cent – in other words to £1,250 each – *simply to bring the value of the portfolio back to where it started.* Needless to say, this would be an enormous handicap which should be avoided at all costs.

Because the performance of the market is made up of hundreds of pluses and minuses, removing the potential major minus of a complete failure puts you well on the way to beating the market.

HIGH YIELDERS' SUPERIOR PERFORMANCE

O'Higgins's second explanation for the consistent out-performance of high-yielders follows from the fact that, almost by definition, these kinds of shares are out of favour with investors. If they were more popular, their share prices would be higher and their dividend yields lower.

The important point about this kind of share is that, often, the poor sentiment surrounding the stock is relatively short-lived. When it is reversed, an investor benefits from the double-whammy of a rising share price (to bring the yield back into line with the rest of the market) and a relatively high income in the meantime. The combination of the two can be very powerful.

You do not need to have been investing for long to realise that the market tends to over-react to both good news and bad. The boom in internet shares in 1999 confirmed that good news and excessive hopes can propel shares to giddy heights; bad news and exaggerated fears, in contrast, can drive them down to bargain-basement levels. The key point is that the market's bouts of extreme optimism and pessimism tend to be reversed in time. When this happens, over-rated glamour stocks can only go one way – downwards – while out-of-favour dogs, which have hit rock-bottom, can only go up. Warren Buffett, the world's most successful investor, said that in the short term the market is a voting machine but in the long run it is a weighing machine. He meant that in the short term the market value of a company is determined by the balance between buyers and sellers but over a longer period it will reflect the true worth of the company.

Do not be misled into thinking that buying out-of-favour high-yielders is a slow or dull way to make money out of shares. Using O'Higgins's method, we selected a portfolio of high-yield shares a few years ago for an investment newsletter we were then writing, *Investing for Growth*. The five shares we chose increased in value over the next 12 months by an average of 39 per cent compared with only 19 per cent for the FTSE 100 as a whole. Two of the five companies were taken over at a significant premium to their price in the market and one of the others doubled in value. When the market changes its mind about an out-of-favour stock, the recovery can be both rapid and substantial.

BENJAMIN GRAHAM'S PARTNER

Benjamin Graham, a legendary American investor, also illustrates the vagaries of the market well. He asks you to imagine that you are in business with a neurotic partner –

the market. Every day your partner names a price at which he is prepared to sell you his share of the business or buy yours.

On some mornings, your partner is feeling on top of the world and offers you a high price for your share; on others, he feels depressed and is prepared to accept a low price for his share. Some days he might only see good news ahead and sometimes prospects for the business seem to him to be extremely gloomy. The key point is that, except perhaps in a very minor way, the underlying value of the business does not change while he is making these wildly fluctuating offers.

The obvious lesson from Graham's analogy is to seek to buy the market, or a particular group of shares within it, when most investors are depressed and the mood is downbeat. More than likely the gloom and doom will have been overdone. One of the best ways of identifying the shares that are out of favour is a high dividend yield. High-yielding shares are also often better backed by assets. This is logical – their lower share prices are nearer to their underlying book values or even standing at a discount to them. It is obviously better to buy shares which are lowly priced due to exaggerated fears than those that are full of the froth of excessive hopes.

FIRMEST ELEMENT OF TOTAL RETURN

The final reason given by O'Higgins for the out-performance of high-yielding shares is that dividends have historically accounted for a large part of the overall return from shares and they are certainly the firmest part of this total return. Research from Barclays Capital has shown that dividends have represented between 40 and 50 per cent of the total return from equities. Just as importantly, because the directors do not cut the payout lightly, they also constitute the most *reliable* part of future returns. You naturally hope that the companies you invest in will make higher profits and pay their shareholders increasing dividends. Fortunately, it is quite possible for a company to make substantial losses for a couple of years or more and *still* pay dividends to its shareholders. The usual reason for directors deciding to maintain a dividend which is not covered by profits is to avoid the stigma of a cut in the payout. Cuts are bad for the share price, weaken market confidence and impair the ability of a company to raise funds in the future. Dividends are, therefore, more stable than company earnings.

THE KEY ELEMENTS OF HIGH-YIELD INVESTING

Here then are the three key reasons why the O'Higgins approach to selecting high-yield shares works so well:

1. The largest companies are least likely to fail completely. By virtually eliminating the potential for a total loss on one of your shares, you are already on the way to beating the market average, which is dragged down by the failures, partial and complete, of many of its constituents.
2. The best value is to be found in shares that are out of favour. These can be most easily identified by a high dividend yield. When the market reassesses the prospects for this kind of company the recovery in share price can be both rapid and substantial. Also, out-of-favour companies are more likely to attract a takeover.
3. Dividends make a very significant contribution to overall investment returns and are by far the safest and

most reliable part of them. Even if the capital value of your high-yield shares only rises in line with other shares, the higher dividend payout will help you gain the crucial extra percentage points of performance that, compounded over time, will transform your wealth.

PUTTING IT INTO PRACTICE

O'Higgins researched several methods for applying his high-yield theory. His principal approaches were:

- to buy the 10 Dow stocks with the highest dividend yield, hold them for a year regardless of developments and then repeat the process for another year
- to select from these 10 high-yield Dow stocks the five with the lowest share prices. Again, the five chosen shares are held for a year regardless of what happens and the process is then repeated
- to buy only the stock with the second-lowest share price from the 10 highest-yielders in the Dow. He calls this the 'penultimate profit prospect'. Again he holds the share for a year.

The total returns (capital growth plus dividends) from the three methods over the 18.5 years of his study are shown in the table below.

	Average annual total return %	Cumulative total %
Ten highest yielders	16.6	1,753
Five high-yield/lowest priced stocks	19.4	2,819
Penultimate profit prospect	24.4	6,245

In comparison with these amazing results, the average annual total return on the Dow over the period was 10.4 per cent, giving a cumulative total return of only 559 per cent, far lower than any of O'Higgins's three methods.

A WORD ABOUT O'HIGGINS'S REFINEMENTS

At first glance the two refinements to the basic approach of picking the 10 highest yielders appear eccentric. Why should either the five lowest-priced shares or the second lowest-priced of the 10 highest yielders be consistently better performers? In fact there is a logic underlying these two refinements to the basic method. The argument for lower prices is that in the US, where bonus share issues are rarer, a low share price usually indicates a smaller market capitalisation. This can be a significant advantage because it is obviously far easier for a relatively small company to double its size than a giant such as BP Amoco. Small companies are therefore more likely to rise by a significant percentage than larger ones.

The logic behind the penultimate profit prospect is that the lowest-priced of the high-yielding shares is quite likely to be a real dog in financial difficulties, whereas the second lowest-priced has in the past often proved to be a company that is simply unpopular at the time.

ADAPTING O'HIGGINS FOR THE UK MARKET

The O'Higgins system for selecting high-yield stocks has had brief periods of popularity in the UK but it is not widely used. This is surprising when you consider the evidence in favour of this simple but effective share-selection method.

The *Financial Times* tested the theory in the UK market between 1979 and 1992. It used the FT 30 index as the base universe of shares from which to select its portfolios. During the 13 years of its test, it found that £10,000, *with gross dividends reinvested*, grew to £130,000 against £81,540 for the same sum invested in the FT-A All Share index.

The authors have tested the system again over a slightly longer 15-year period from 1984 to 1998 with similarly favourable results. In particular, the aim was to see whether O'Higgins's Penultimate Profit Prospect would work here. It also provided an opportunity to see how well the high-yielders worked on their own, and compared with the performance of the lowest-yielders.

In addition to answering these questions, the object was to develop a system that was both accessible and user-friendly to the small ISA investor who wanted to go one step beyond a tracker fund but did not want to spend too much time worrying about his or her investments.

For this reason, the top 30 companies from the FTSE 100 were taken rather than the now more obscure FT 30 index. These shares can be traded in volume and are among the safest and most secure in the UK.

The key results of the authors' tests are shown in the table opposite. The sources of the data and the methodology are explained in Appendix II.

TEN HIGHEST YIELDERS

As you can see from the table, the compound rate of total return from the FT-A All Share index was 17.1 per cent over the 15-year period ended 31 December 1998. This is a very good performance that is difficult to beat consistently. However, the 10 highest-yielders gave a

Summary of Annual Returns for Portfolios Developed from the FTSE 100 Top 30 Companies by Market Value for the 15-Year Period 1984–98

YEAR ENDING 31st December	All-share %	Top 30 %	10 Highest Yielders of Top 30 %	10 Lowest Yielders of Top 30 %	Highest Yielder of Top 30 %	Second Highest Yielder of Top 30 %	Second Lowest Priced of 10 Highest Yielders %	5 Lowest Priced of 10 Highest Yielders %	5 Lowest Mkt Value of 10 Highest Yielders %
1984	32.0	28.6	36.9	35.8	29.2	32.8	103.2	47.0	32.4
1985	20.1	16.3	28.9	5.7	24.2	51.8	30.4	43.0	38.8
1986	27.5	26.6	41.5	19.0	38.9	56.2	52.4	40.1	41.5
1987	8.0	7.3	5.6	10.2	11.1	14.9	3.3	4.8	0.4
1988	11.5	8.4	5.1	3.8	5.7	12.0	21.5	8.4	3.4
1989	36.1	45.9	47.3	50.8	15.3	48.7	62.4	46.5	42.3
1990	-9.7	-6.8	-12.1	-6.7	-17.2	5.1	-19.3	-8.3	-16.7
1991	20.7	31.5	21.4	47.3	12.5	48.2	16.0	22.3	22.8
1992	20.5	24.2	25.6	17.9	54.5	-10.4	48.2	34.3	26.4
1993	28.4	18.2	38.3	6.7	70.8	60.1	49.3	38.1	47.4
1994	-5.9	-5.0	-7.5	-3.4	-8.8	-2.9	-2.9	-8.2	-6.4
1995	23.8	21.8	16.8	20.8	-9.6	7.7	18.0	6.6	21.6
1996	16.6	14.2	11.4	20.9	-20.2	-4.1	-4.1	1.6	7.6
1997	23.5	35.1	41.4	27.7	24.2	28.5	-24.5	33.4	40.4
1998	13.7	16.4	13.1	30.7	-3.2	-2.7	-13.6	27.4	2.0
Compound return	**17.1**	**18.0**	**19.6**	**18.0**	**12.4**	**22.7**	**18.2**	**20.9**	**18.6**

compound annual total return of 19.6 per cent. Even this small outperformance can make a significant difference over the medium to long term.

In the 15 years to 1998 it certainly made its mark – the cumulative return was 1,356 per cent against 966 per cent for the FT-A All Share Index. The 10 highest-yielders also handsomely beat a basket of the top 30 shares which grew at a compound rate of 18 per cent over the period to give a cumulative return of 1,101 per cent.

We also tested the 10 lowest-yielders (mainly very well-known growth stocks of the time like Vodafone, Zeneca and Reuters). Despite performing consistently well during the recent bull market, their average overall return was no better than the top 30 at 18 per cent.

FIVE LOWEST-PRICED/HIGHEST-YIELDERS

Now let us look at the five lowest-priced of the top 10 highest-yielding companies. Here the results are even more impressive over the 15-year period. The compound return of 20.9 per cent is almost four percentage points better than the FT-A All Share index. After 15 years, a £1,000 investment in the five shares selected using this method would have grown to be worth £17,227. A similar £1,000 investment in the FT-A All Share index would have grown to only £10,655.

The results are also more consistent. The five lowest-priced high-yielders would have beaten the FT-A All Share index in 10 of the 15 years and in only two of the five underperforming years was the shortfall of any significance.

It is interesting to note that after these two bad years, 1995 and 1996, the method enjoyed two years of excellent performance. The gain of 33.4 per cent in 1997 compared with a 23.5 per cent rise in the FT-A All Share, while in 1998 the 27.4 per cent total return was exactly twice the 13.7 per cent from the market.

THE PENULTIMATE PROFIT PROSPECT

On the face of it, the second lowest-priced of the 10 highest-yielders would have been a good selection on average. Its cumulative return of 1,122 per cent compared favourably with both the All Share and the top 30. However, on closer examination its success was very dependent on one exceptional year way back in 1984 and in more recent years it has been very disappointing.

In the days of single-company PEPs there was a strong incentive for investors to try to identify a particularly attractive single share but, with the advent of ISAs, there is no need to put all your eggs in one basket. Some years, the Penultimate Profit Prospect will do exceptionally well, but the risk of failure is too high. In four out of the last five years of our study, for example, this share had a negative total return.

If you do decide to go for a one-share selection (for example, if you still have a single company PEP) a far more consistently successful approach has been to select the second highest-yielder from the top 30 shares. Although this fell in three of the last five years of the study, the declines were marginal while the rises in the other two years were very impressive. The cumulative return for the second highest-yielder over 15 years was 2,058 per cent, the highest return of all the methods tested.

What sort of companies produced this high average return, beating the FT-A All Share in 11 of the 15 years under review? Here is the list:

The Second Highest Yielders of Top 30 Companies

Year	Company	Total return (%)	FT-A All Share total return (%)
1984	Imperial Group	32.8	32.0
1985	Imperial Group	51.8	20.1
1986	Shell	56.2	27.5
1987	British Gas	14.9	8.0
1988	Barclays	12.0	11.5
1989	Barclays	48.7	36.1
1990	BP	5.1	−9.7
1991	ICI	48.2	20.7
1992	BP	−10.4	20.5
1993	ICI	60.1	28.4
1994	British Gas	−2.9	−5.9
1995	BAT	37.7	23.8
1996	British Gas	−4.1	16.6
1997	BT	28.5	23.5
1998	Rio Tinto	−2.7	13.7

There is some logic to support the proposition that the second highest-yielder should produce better results than the highest. The highest-yielding company could be a real dog which will prove unable to sustain its very high dividend payment. The second-highest has a better chance of simply being a company that is unpopular at the time. On balance, however, other than for old single company PEPs, more cautious investors should avoid focusing their investments in this way. The performance of the five-share portfolios has been consistently good so it is pointless to take such a large and unnecessary risk.

SPECIMEN PORTFOLIOS

As you can see from the table of figures, 1997 and 1998 were good years for the O'Higgins approach in the UK, so let us look at the two portfolios that would have been selected in those years using the five lowest-priced of the 10 highest-yielders:

1997

	Yield %
BT	6.0
BTR	4.8
BG	4.8
Grand Metropolitan	4.8
Guinness	4.9

1998

	Yield %
Shell	4.0
BT	5.1
Diageo	4.8
BAT	6.0
GEC	4.5

At the beginning of 1997, the market still viewed BT as a rather dull telephone stock but over the ensuing two years the benefit to the company of the explosive growth in internet traffic became increasingly apparent. In 1997, BT's shares rose 23 per cent while in 1998 they almost doubled, rising by 92 per cent, an extraordinary performance for a company of BT's size. The merger of Grand Metropolitan and Guinness added spice to the 1997 portfolio, with the shares up 32 per cent and 25 per cent respectively. This more than made up for BTR, which fell 29 per cent as industrial conglomerates became the dinosaurs of the investment world.

Hindsight is, of course, a wonderful thing in investment and the subsequent performance of BT showed that most good things tend to come to an end. And if BT made that point, GEC proved it in spades in its subsequent incarnation as Marconi.

In 1998, GEC played an impressive second fiddle to BT, rising 31 per cent as George Simpson began the process of transforming a well-run but dull conglomerate into a new-economy telecommunications company for the 21st century. Over-expansion at the height of the tech boom, however, brought that house of cards tumbling down.

The crash did not come, however, until after a fantastic period of share price growth. And the beauty of the O'Higgins method is that the annual rejigging of the portfolio naturally throws out shares which have become over-valued because their dividend yields fall away as their share prices rise.

The other attraction of these two portfolios is that they also offer a reasonable spread of investment. In 1998, for example, the shares covered oil, telecoms, drinks, tobacco and electronics. The same method in early 2002 produced a portfolio heavily biased towards the banking sector – it included the following shares:

Company	Yield (%)
HSBC	4.6
HBOS	3.8
Lloyds TSB	5.0
Prudential	3.5
BAT	5.2

CAVEATS

An important point arising from our research is the consistency of the performance, especially of the five-share lowest-priced portfolios. During the 15 years, the worst performance was an 8 per cent decline, while the highest was a 47 per cent increase. There were twice as many years in which the portfolio outperformed the All Share index as underperformed it.

However, the research does not prove that the same kind of performance can be achieved in the future. *Shares can go down as well as up and there is a strong possibility that there might be several years in succession when the system will not work.* There is also a chance, albeit slim, of one of the top 30 companies failing completely or suffering such a major setback that it materially affects performance. With a five-share portfolio, as we have seen, this would have a dramatic impact. With a one-share portfolio, it would be disastrous.

Because this method only requires you to buy shares once a year, dealing costs are not a major consideration. However, because the selection process is mechanised, you do not receive advice and should, therefore, use an execution-only broker.

HOW TO SELECT SHARES FOR THE SYSTEM

Selecting shares for any of the O'Higgins methods is very simple, although early in 2002 the only paper which listed the leading companies together with their dividend yields and share prices was *The Sunday Times*.

Using our adaptation of the method, you are interested only in the 30 companies with the largest market capitalisations. *The Sunday Times* lists the top 200 companies together with each company's rank by market capitalisation and its dividend yield. Unfortunately it lists them alphabetically so you will have to do a little preliminary legwork by manually drawing up a list of the largest 30 companies on a separate sheet, together with their dividend yields and share prices.

Now take your list and use it to draw up a list of the 10 highest-yielding shares. The best way to do this is to pick a dividend yield figure that is obviously too low to qualify for the top 10 yield shortlist and draw a line through any company with a yield below this figure. It is then an easy task to eliminate any further shares, as necessary, to leave you with your shortlist of the 10 highest-yielders out of the top 30 companies. These are the shares you want to buy if you intend to follow the basic O'Higgins high-yield system. Over the past 15 years this has beaten the market by 2.5 per cent per annum, resulting in a cumulative 37 per cent outperformance during that period.

If you decide instead to opt for O'Higgins's more refined method, you cross off from the list of high-yielders the five with the highest share prices. The remaining five shares are the recommended portfolio for the O'Higgins highest-yield/lowest-price method of investing. This is the system that beat the UK market by 3.8 per cent a year between 1984 and 1998. The cumulative outperformance in this case was a much more impressive 62 per cent. As you can see, after a difficult period in 1995 and 1996, it excelled in 1997 and 1998 – and this raises another important point. Do not judge performance over a one- or two-year period. It is the long term you are interested in.

If you have a single-company PEP left over from before the change over to ISAs you may be interested in using it to shelter an investment in the second highest-yielder.

Simply choose the appropriate share from your list of 10 high-yielders. The second highest-yielder has outperformed the market, over the past 15 years, by a substantial 5.6 per cent a year.

As you can see, it is a remarkably simple exercise to select a system portfolio or a single share using our adaptation of the O'Higgins method. You do not even have to know anything about the companies in question. Once a year you repeat the whole process, when you will find that a few shares need to be replaced. For investors who want to beat the market averages with a minimum of effort, this is the most attractive share selection method.

SUMMARY

1. O'Higgins's methods seem to work both in America and the UK for the following reasons:

   a) There is a strong element of contrary thinking in buying high-yielding shares. Going against the crowd in this way has been shown to be an effective way of beating the market.

   b) Dividends are a major part of overall market returns.

   c) Leading companies are less likely to fail completely, giving you an important edge over the market.

   d) Lower-priced shares are subject to larger percentage movements.

2. It is easy to select shares using the O'Higgins principle with *The Sunday Times*. The selection process takes no more than an hour or so and needs to be repeated only once a year.

3. Adapted for the UK, the O'Higgins approach, *based on*

an extended 15-year test period, seems to offer better than average returns. The two main methods for a portfolio of shares are:

a) The ten highest-yielders from the top 30 companies. This system produced a 19.6 per cent compound annual return against 17.1 per cent for the UK market.

b) The five lowest-priced shares from the ten highest-yielders. This produced 20.9 per cent against the market's 17.1 per cent.

The difference of 3.8 per cent a year for the refined method may not seem very much but a £1,000 annual investment in the five shares using that method would have produced £17,227 in 15 years compared with only £10,625 from the FT-A All Share index.

4. The capital gains and income from the portfolio should be sheltered from taxation to the maximum possible extent as explained in Chapter 7.

5. For owners of single company PEPs, the second highest-yielder of the 10 highest-yielders seems to offer above-average returns. In our 15-year test, it produced 22.7 per cent per annum against the market's 17.1 per cent.

6. Use an execution-only broker to keep your costs as low as possible.

7. There is no guarantee that O'Higgins's methods will work as well in the future as they have in the past. One of the companies selected could fail or suffer a major setback, which could have a dramatic effect on a small portfolio. There is no such thing as a completely fail-safe system for investing in equities. However, by going against the crowd, you dramatically increase your margin of safety and your chance of long-term success.

8. Do not judge the performance of your high-yielders on
   one year's results alone. In some years they do not fare
   as well as the market, but in the long term the method
   seems to work well, providing an above-average overall
   return.

10

MORE ACTIVE INVESTMENT

'Forecasts are dangerous, particularly those about the future.'

Samuel Goldwyn

Becoming a millionaire and securing financial freedom for yourself and your family are achievable even if you know little about stock market investment. As long as you start early enough, the magical power of compounding ensures that the returns from tracker funds or a mechanistic high-yield investment approach will make you relatively rich. However, if you want to be more certain of achieving significant wealth through the stock market you will need to devote some time and effort to becoming a successful active investor. The good news is that investing in this way is both lucrative and great fun.

Most people are vaguely aware that a greater investment return is only achievable with the adoption of a greater degree of risk. Because they misunderstand the nature of risk, however, they tend to err unnecessarily on the side of caution. For example, they leave their savings in a building society account rather than investing in the stock market, accepting a much lower return in exchange for a perceived lower degree of risk.

Even if they realise that *in the long term* the stock market is not more risky than other savings vehicles, most investors prefer to shelter within the perceived safe haven of a managed fund and never give themselves the chance of benefiting from the spectacular gains that can be achieved by investing directly in shares.

For many people a more cautious approach is appropriate. If you have neither the time nor the inclination to learn more about investment you should stick to tracker funds or the systematic high-yield approach outlined in Chapter 9. You can still achieve relative wealth and financial freedom in this way as long as you start early enough, are disciplined about saving regularly and plan your tax affairs sensibly.

However, reduction in risk comes at a price. The wide spread of investments in a pooled fund necessarily means that the high potential gains available in the stock market are diluted. If a fund holds 100 shares of equal value, for example, a doubling in the price of any one of them will increase the value of the whole portfolio by only 1 per cent. In a portfolio of only 10 shares, each with the same initial value, the same doubling of one stock would increase the value of the portfolio by 10 per cent.

Another important point to bear in mind is that a fund manager with a portfolio of 100 shares will know very little about most of the stocks. He insures against his lack of knowledge by buying a wide spread of investments. If one of his shares loses half its value, the value of the fund is reduced by a relatively insignificant 0.5 per cent and he keeps his well-paid job.

The active investor adopts a different approach. By restricting himself to only 10 or 20 shares, he stands a good chance of knowing them all intimately. Unlike the fund manager, he is prepared to accept the risk that one of his shares might seriously damage the short-term performance of the whole portfolio in exchange for knowing that one good choice will materially improve his overall performance. This is especially true if he runs profits and cuts losses.

MARGIN OF SAFETY

The key to successful active investment is to establish a margin of safety. This maximises the chance of benefiting from the greater upside potential of a small, carefully selected portfolio of shares while at the same time minimising the downside risks of this narrower choice of stocks.

To achieve this margin of safety, it is vital to invest using a method. Your method might change in response to varying market conditions and investment fashions, but it is crucial that when you make an investment you know *exactly why you are making it*. This will provide you with an important edge over most investors who often invest in an amateurish way. Buying shares on a whim, or because someone gives you a tip is a sure way to lose money. If you are going to approach active investment in this dilettante way you would be much better off sticking with a tracker fund or the enforced discipline of the high-yield method.

The previous chapter explained this high-yield approach, which is an excellent *passive* investment method. This chapter and the next will show you some of the main approaches to more *active* investment and point you in the right direction to learn more about them. Becoming a successful active investor is a continuing learning process and these two chapters will give only a taste of what lies ahead if you decide to take your financial future into your own hands in this way.

It is hoped you will do so for two reasons. First, by

accepting the greater risk of active investment you are very likely to enjoy *significantly* greater returns. As we have seen, even a small outperformance each year can make a material difference to your long-term wealth. Second, the investment game is great fun. By becoming an active investor you will join a fast-growing group of people for whom securing financial freedom is not a necessary chore but an enjoyable and at times exhilarating pastime.

GAINING AN EDGE

It is only worthwhile becoming an active investor if you can gain an edge over other investors. Otherwise, the time and energy devoted to understanding investment and selecting shares would be far better spent in some other more productive way.

You might think that the difference between performing averagely and performing better than averagely is mainly a matter of luck. Of course, luck plays its part but, as in most games, the skilful players always win in the end. They make sure that they have a competitive edge and their success naturally follows.

HOW TO WIN AT MONOPOLY

The incidence of luck and skill is illustrated by a popular game that almost everybody knows well. Many people would argue that luck is what matters in Monopoly and there is no doubt that you will always lose if you throw appalling dice while your opponents throw well. However, over a long period, the luck in dice-throwing evens out and the persistent use of skill establishes a winning edge.

The first important use of skill in Monopoly is deciding which sites to buy. Getting this aspect of the game right can make all the difference, but most people do not give it a second thought. To determine what makes some sites much better than others you need to do some arithmetic to calculate which are likely to give you the best return. First, add up the cost of each colour group of sites – the dark greens, for example, Regent Street (£300), Oxford Street (£300) and Bond Street (£320), total £920 while the light blues, Angel Islington (£100), Euston Road (£100) and Pentonville Road (£120), cost £320. Then add the cost of building hotels on each colour group. In the case of the dark greens, the cost of each house is £200 and you need to have four houses before being allowed to build a hotel for an extra charge of £200. The total cost of each hotel is, therefore, £1,000 on each site, giving a grand total for the dark green group of £3,920 (3 × £1,000 + £920).

The light blue group is much cheaper – houses cost only £50 each, with an extra £50 for hotels. The cost of the three hotels is, therefore, £750 and, with £320 for the three sites, this gives a grand total of only £1,070.

Finally, calculate your rental return on the two groups, assuming that you have built hotels. To do this, add the hotel rents together and express them as a percentage of the total building and land cost. In the case of the dark green sites, the rental on Regent Street and Oxford Street is £1,275 and on Bond Street £1,400. The total rent is, therefore, £3,950, which is just over the total cost of £3,920, giving a percentage yield of 101 per cent.

The three light blue sites have hotel rents totalling £1,700, which on the total outlay of only £1,070 makes them a much better proposition with a much higher percentage return of 159 per cent.

Refining the criteria

You might think from all this that the light blue sites are
the most attractive. Their 159 per cent return is by far the
best of them all and the dark greens' 101 per cent is the
worst. But there is more to it than that. Success in
Monopoly is a product of two factors – the rental return on
the sites you own and the frequency with which your
opponents land on them. To gain the ultimate winning
edge, you have to know which sites the other players are
most likely to land on.

As it happens, the orange group, Bow Street, Marlborough
Street and Vine Street, are the most visited sites. First,
players frequently go to Jail and the three orange sites are a
likely dice throw away, waiting to welcome your opponents
on their return to freedom. Even if the ex-prisoners throw a
low number, there is still a chance of landing on one of the
orange sites on their next throw.

Also, the Chance cards 'Advance to Pall Mall' and
'Advance to Marylebone Station' both bypass the light blue
and other sites and leave your opponents ready to land on
your orange hotels. Finally, there is another Chance card,
'Go back three spaces', which from one position lands your
opponents on Vine Street.

The rental return on the orange sites is second highest
of all at 141 per cent and, with the much greater likelihood
of landing on them, the player with all three orange sites
is favourite to win. Acquiring them should, therefore, be
your main strategic aim. There are a few other tricks of the
trade, like keeping a prudent cash reserve, mortgaging
isolated sites before bartering them and building houses
and hotels on completed sites as fast as possible. The key
point we want to make is that any player who adopts this
kind of systematic approach is, *over a period*, more likely

to win more often. No-one can budget for the dice, but everyone can adopt the best strategic approach.

MOVING UP THE SCALE

The luck/skill ratio in Monopoly has been explained in some detail because the game is a simple one and we can all relate to it. There are, however, many other games of chance with a much higher degree of skill. Going up the scale several notches, backgammon is a game you should not play for money unless you have read a book or two and understand the odds of rolling each combination of the dice, the importance of timing and back games, the key points on the board and, most important of all, when to offer a double and when to accept one.

Without some knowledge of these key factors, you might as well give your money to someone who does know about them, as their extra skill will be applied on every move and, cumulatively, will soon overcome the luck of the dice.

Going up the scale still further, bridge is an infinitely more complicated game and a continual (and very enjoyable) learning experience. Once again, good players know the odds of suits breaking and finesses. They also understand squeezes, end plays and the like, and know exactly which cards you have in your hand as the play of each contract nears its end.

Bridge is comparable to stock market investment because the elements of luck and skill have a similar balance in both. Just as, in bridge, there is nothing you can do about the cards you are dealt, in investment there is nothing you can do about the state of the market as a whole.

Warren Buffett admits he does not know which way the market is going, so there is no point in the average investor trying to outguess everyone else. However, you can dramatically improve your chances of being a successful investor whatever the market does by applying the same systematic approach that distinguishes the good bridge player. It is no coincidence that Warren Buffett enjoys the game and plays it on the internet. Even if the market moves against you, the important thing is to continue 'playing' and developing your investment skills. Be patient and persistent and, over time, as the market recovers, your skill will reward you generously.

TEN WAYS TO GAIN AN EDGE

There are ten ways you can gain an edge over other investors:

1. **Use the 80/20 rule**
   The 80/20 rule states that in most fields of human endeavour, 80 per cent of the effort expended results in only 20 per cent of the benefits gained. The converse is also true – 20 per cent of the best-directed effort can produce 80 per cent of the benefit. There is no need to become an expert on the 80 per cent of investment theory that you will never require. Instead focus on the 20 per cent that will be explained in detail.

2. **Choose a method that suits you**
   It is important that the method of investment you choose to focus on should suit your temperament and character. The two methods we will outline in the next chapter share some common features but they appeal to different types of investor. One approach, for example, is to select reasonably priced shares in companies

which are growing their profits at an above-average rate. These companies may have ambitions to be the market leaders of tomorrow but today they are often small and relatively obscure. This approach suits some investors but others might worry about their savings being tied up in companies that are not household names and could, *in extremis*, fail.

If you are more cautious and worried by the prospect of entrusting your savings to these small companies, you might prefer another method which focuses on out-of-favour blue-chip shares with household names.

As a first step, you should read an excellent book, *Selecting Shares That Perform*, by Richard Koch. He outlines 10 methods of investment in sufficient detail for you to get a broad idea of the one that is most likely to suit you.

3. **Apply the Zulu Principle**

The third key competitive edge you should develop is to become a *relative* expert. We call this concept the Zulu Principle. Once you have narrowed the focus sufficiently, you can quickly learn more about a given subject than the vast majority of people. The idea came from a four-page article about Zulus in *Reader's Digest*. Anyone who read it would have immediately known more about Zulus than most other people. If they were then to have visited the local library and read all the available books on the subject they would certainly have known more about the subject than anyone in their town or county. A visit to South Africa with a few months spent on a Zulu kraal, followed by reading all of the available literature on Zulus at a South African university, would without doubt have made them one of the leading experts in the world.

The point is that the history of Zulus and their culture today is a relatively narrow and defined area of study. *By investing a disproportionate time in the subject, almost anyone could become an acknowledged authority on it.*

The same principle applies to certain aspects of investment. You will be shown two narrow and defined areas of active investment in which, with further laser-beam application, you can become *a relative expert.* Picking one of these methods, or another you will find and develop, and then focusing on it, will give you a crucial edge over most investors whose approach tends to be unfocused and, therefore, comparatively ineffective.

4. **Join an investment club**

Investment can be a lonely business, but if you join an investment club, especially as a novice investor, you will obtain help and sometimes inspiration from the other private investors who are members. The meetings, usually once a month, can be fun too and should help to improve the performance of your own shares as well as the communal fund managed by the club.

The legal maximum for members is 20. Members might include the manager of a restaurant, a solicitor, an accountant, an estate agent and perhaps someone in public relations. Every one of these people brings to the group their own area of expertise and experience and helps to widen the group's circle of competence by adding their know-how to its overall strength.

You could argue that if you join an investment club, you will not acquire an edge over the other investors in the club. This is true, but you will at least keep level with them and your shared knowledge will give you an edge over investors who do not belong to a club.

There are other advantages too. Within every club there is always a 'faster gun' – someone who knows more about investment than the other members and can add to the knowledge of the group. Also, in a club it is easier to stick to a discipline and to gain moral support from talking about problems with other members. Last but not least, the cost of newsletters and other necessary investment services such as *Company REFS* can be shared to reduce the expense to a very affordable level per member.

Anyone interested in joining an investment club, or forming one, should contact ProShare, Centurion House, 24 Monument Street, London EC3R 8AQ (tel: 020 7394 5200). In particular, they should obtain a copy of the ProShare manual, which costs £29.50 and explains everything they need to know.

5. **Subscribe to a leading newsletter or online investment service, preferably one with an educational aspect**
    There are a few worthwhile investment newsletters. *Small Company Sharewatch* and *The AIM Newsletter* are particularly good. For investors who are particularly interested in the high-technology sector there is nothing to beat *Techinvest*.

    More recently printed newsletters have been rather superseded by online or email services, which have the advantage of immediacy – they can send a share tip or update to their subscribers almost instantaneously while their printed rivals are tied into inflexible production schedules and weekly or monthly deadlines.

    Tom Stevenson currently edits an email newsletter – Hemscott Analyst – which sends regular share tips and other investment advice including searches of the Hemscott database of UK quoted companies, interviews with leading fund managers and other articles of general investment interest. At the time of writing, Hemscott Analyst's tips have outperformed the market by a substantial margin. A free trial is available by signing up at www.hemscott.net/analyst.

6. **Read a number of books on investment by leading experts**
Investment is no different from any other specialist subject like cooking, gardening or golf. If you wanted to be a better cook, gardener or golfer, you would try to get plenty of practice but you would also seek out books written by the experts who devote their lives to these pursuits.

First, you must make sure you understand the basics of investment so good primers are your first port of call. *The Beginners Guide to Investment* by Bernard Gray and *How to Read the Financial Pages* by Michael Brett are both first class and should give you a good grounding. You should then round this off with Bernice Cohen's excellent book *The Armchair Investor* and Jim Slater's *Investment Made Easy*. Still at the beginner's level, we recommend you to read *Accounts Demystified* by Anthony Rice. This excellent book will help you to understand company accounts in a very simple way.

In the UK, there is a growing number of investment books by British authors but we still depend to a large extent on imports from America. When you consider that some of these books are written by investment giants like Peter Lynch, Kenneth Fisher and Martin Zweig, or are detailed accounts of the lives and methods of legendary investors like Warren Buffett, it is absurd not to spend a little time drinking from the fountains of their expertise. In some cases, a lifetime's experience is packed into a couple of books. The time spent reading any of them should be handsomely rewarded by improved investment performance in the years ahead.

In the panel on the following three pages we have listed the books we recommend in three categories in order of ease of reading and pertinence to your objective. Almost all of them are available in paperback.

There are a number of other well-known books like *The Intelligent Investor* and *Security Analysis* but they are too advanced at this stage and you may never need to get around to them. If you read even four or five of the books recommended, you will put yourself well ahead of most other UK investors.

7. **Keep in daily touch with your shares**
Once you have acquired some shares, it is crucial that you keep in touch with them and also maintain a vigilant watch for new investment opportunities. As a bare minimum, you should read the *Financial Times* and one other quality broadsheet every day. The Saturday *FT* is particularly useful for investors. On a weekly basis, you should also read *Investors Chronicle* and a newer weekly magazine, *Shares*, which is also a good source of ideas.

No discussion of investment information can now exclude the internet. It is a cornucopia of financial data and company information. Many of the facts and figures which until recently were the preserve of City professionals are now available free on the internet. To begin with, the following sites are recommended, but new ones are popping up almost daily:

INVESTMENT BOOKS

For Growth Investors

1. *The Zulu Principle* by Jim Slater. There are chapters on the common characteristics of growth shares and the criteria for selecting them; the price-earnings growth factor; cash flow; competitive advantage and relative strength. There are also chapters on the essential requirements for investing in shells, turnarounds, cyclical and asset situations.

2. *One Up On Wall Street* by Peter Lynch. An excellent and very readable book by one of America's most successful mutual fund managers.

3. *Beating The Street* by Peter Lynch. Another excellent book full of practical advice.

4. *The Midas Touch* by John Train. An excellent brief outline of the investment principles that have made Warren Buffett America's leading investor.

5. *Midas Investing* by Jonathan Steinberg. The author, who has won the Wall Street journal's stockpicking contest many times, explains his five-part stock selection method. His key criteria include momentum, insider buying and PEGs.

6. *How to Make Money in Stocks* by William O'Neill. Includes many good investment ideas, in particular the author's CANSLIM formula for stock selection.

7. *Beyond the Zulu Principle* by Jim Slater. A more advanced explanation and update on the ideas outlined in *The Zulu Principle*.

8. *Common Stocks and Uncommon Profits* by Philip Fisher. This classic work on growth stocks was first published in 1958. Even Benjamin Graham, the dean of value investing, recommended it to growth stock investors.

For Value Investors

1. *Contrarian Investment Strategies: The Next Generation* by David Dreman. A truly excellent and classic book on contrarian investment.
2. *Super Stocks* by Kenneth Fisher. A superb guide to buying high technology stocks that have experienced a setback and are due for a massive recovery in their share prices. In particular, the author explains in detail how to use price-to-sales and price-to-research and development ratios.
3. *On Investing* by John Neff. A great book on value investment by one of America's best fund managers. In particular, he explains the ins and outs of buying shares on low price–earnings ratios.

For All Investors

1. *Selecting Shares that Perform* by Richard Koch. An outline of '10 ways that work'. An excellent primer for investors who want to understand the full range of methods of investment available before choosing the one that suits their temperament.
2. *Extraordinary Popular Delusions and the Madness of Crowds* by Charles Mackay. First published in 1841 – a classic on crowd psychology.
3. *The Stockmarket* by John Littlewood. Reviews the last 50 years of capitalism at work and examines issues such as the rise in power of the shareholder, the power of technology, privatisation and the link between the stock market and wider forces at work in the economy.
4. *The Craft of Investing* by John Train. Explains in an easy-to-understand way growth investing, value investing and investing in emerging markets,

including when to buy and sell and how to avoid losing strategies.

5. *Beating The Dow* by Michael O'Higgins and John Downes. A detailed exposition of Dow stocks and the high yield method of buying them when they are out of favour to produce returns that dwarf the market averages.

6. *Accounting for Growth* by Terry Smith. An excellent book on accounting practices that should help you to detect when creative accounting has been at work.

7. *Interpreting Company Reports and Accounts* by Holmes and Sugden. This book is a must for active private investors who want to understand fully the mysteries and complexities of company accounts. It is constantly being updated so make sure that you buy the most recent edition.

8. *Charters on Charting* by David Charters. The author explains in simple language why he believes that charting works and gives precise details of how to do it yourself.

9. *Winning on Wall Street* by Martin Zweig. The famous American guru outlines his investment philosophy and measures for stock selection and market forecasting.

10. *What Works on Wall Street* by James O'Shaughnessy. A fascinating study of the investment strategies that have worked best over the past 40 years. The author examines investment criteria one by one to establish which of them have been the most effective. Positive relative strength and low price-to-sales ratios emerge as the winners.

www.hemscott.net provides access to a wealth of investment data, daily comment from Hemscott's in-house team of journalists headed by Tom Stevenson, a news service from the AFX agency and full releases from the Regulatory News Service of the Stock Exchange. All news stories are extensively cross-referenced to Hemscott's database. There are details of brokers' forecasts and directors' dealings as well as commentary on companies and sectors in the news. A full news archive puts the latest stories into context.

The Hemscott 'Information Exchange', is one of the most widely used internet bulletin boards. These are forums for private and professional investors alike to swap information about companies. A great deal of the postings on these sites is trivial and lightweight, but if you are prepared to sift through there are occasionally some very well-informed and well-researched comments.

www.ft.com is the primary internet site for the Financial Times group. Linked to the main site is www.ftyour money.com, a personal finance site and www.ftinvestor .com, which focuses on the markets and investment. There is a wealth of information here, including access to the FT's valuable archives. The navigation round the site is, however, not very user-friendly.

www.fool.co.uk is the UK arm of the cult American website *The Motley Fool*. A good source of irreverent comment on the investment scene.

www.citywire.co.uk is a news service which can be a good source of investment ideas and is especially useful for early guidance on stake-building by influential investors.

www.news.bbc.co.uk is an excellent source of up to the minute news, with a good business news section.

www.bloomberg.com is an excellent source of data on the US market. Even if you are not investing directly in American shares, it is worth keeping an eye on events over the pond – as the old adage says, when Wall Street sneezes London catches a cold.

Investment information and the internet are tailor-made for each other because of the high volume of statistical data which requires constant updating. The internet is the perfect medium for disseminating this kind of information in a cost-effective way and it is very easy now to keep in daily touch with all of your shares. You do not want to be the last person to hear of important announcements like substantial directors' dealings, annual or interim results, trading statements, takeovers and revisions to brokers' consensus forecasts. Now, through the internet, the private investor can for the first time enjoy a level playing field with the professional.

8. **Obtain a reliable source of statistical and other information**
   One of the major reasons we have highlighted the O'Higgins approach to high-yield stocks as a kind of half-way house between passive tracker fund investing and active investment is that it is so easy to put into practice.
   Selecting stocks using either of the more active methods we will explain in the next chapter is more complicated and requires access to a database of financial information. Fortunately, technology has

come to the rescue and this kind of information is now relatively easily and cheaply available.

Until recently, computerised searches of stock market databases were the preserve of the professional investor, but in this area too the playing field has been levelled in favour of the active private investor. To gain a real edge over the market and other investors, you need to arm yourself with some basic tools of the trade, the most important of which is a remarkable investment product – REFS, now available in book and CD form and, most usefully, on the internet.

REFS is a computerised search and select tool for shares. It was devised by Jim Slater and is published in CD form by HS Financial Publishing, the publications arm of the former Hemmington Scott which is now a subsidiary of Charterhouse Communications. The online version, which has the merit of being updated daily, is available via www.hemscott.net. REFS is a database of statistical information on around 1,700 quoted companies which can be interrogated on the basis of criteria which you select.

It can be used, for example, to produce a list of companies with a price-earnings ratio of less than 15. This list can then be further interrogated to produce a list of shares with both a PER of less than 15 and earnings growth of more than say 20 per cent. Further self-selected criteria can be applied in turn until you arrive at a manageable short list of potential investments. It is very quick, accurate and can be used just as well for selecting growth and value shares. The authors use Online REFS every day and cannot imagine investment life without it.

If you do not want to subscribe to REFS on your own, you should team up with a group of other investors or

join an investment club to share the cost. It will soon
repay your initial outlay with investment opportunities
that you would never have come across otherwise.

9. **Cut your losses and run your profits**

   There are many famous investment adages you will
   learn as you read more about the subject. One of them
   stands out from the others like a beacon – 'Cut your
   losses and run your profits'. This is, of course, against
   human nature but nevertheless totally logical.

   If you always identify as soon as possible and then
   acknowledge your mistakes by selling if necessary at a
   loss, your losses will tend to be small as a result.
   Conversely, if you run your profits they will tend to be
   large and, in a few wonderful cases, gigantic.

   It is often hard to hold on to a share that has doubled
   or trebled and equally hard to acknowledge a mistake
   and cut a loss, sometimes in very short order. However,
   it is the key to successful investment, especially with
   growth shares which have such enormous upside
   potential if you choose them wisely.

10. **Monitor your investment performance**

    As with any activity, some people are better at investment
    than others. If you find after a year or two of active invest-
    ment that you are not keeping up with the market you
    should probably stick to tracker fund or systematic high-
    yield investing. As we have seen, both of these methods
    should be sufficiently productive to help you reach your
    goal of becoming a millionaire and achieving financial
    freedom. If you find active investment is not successful or
    fun, put your time to better use.

SUMMARY

1. Active investment is the only way to expose yourself fully to the fantastic potential gains from the stock market. By investing directly in a relatively narrow portfolio of shares, you run the risk that a poor choice will inflict damage on your overall investment performance but it is the only way to avoid the benefit of an excellent investment decision being diluted away.

2. The active investor must adopt a method so that he or she is always fully aware of why a particular share has been purchased. Never buy shares on a whim or just because a friend tips them to you.

3. The best active investment methods share a margin of safety. This limits the downside potential and provides the rationale for the upside.

4. Gain an edge with these ten common sense steps:

    i) Follow the 80/20 rule. Do not waste time on what you do not need to know about investment.

    ii) Choose an investment method that suits your temperament and character.

    iii) Use the Zulu Principle and adopt a laser-beam approach to learning about your chosen method of investment.

    iv) Join an investment club to widen your circle of competence and learn from other investors. Also, try to attend an occasional investment conference.

    v) Subscribe to a leading newsletter, preferably one with an educational approach.

    vi) Read a number of books on investment by leading experts, especially those about your chosen investment method.

    vii) Keep in daily touch with your shares through

newspapers, your stockbroker and the internet.

viii) Obtain a reliable source of statistical and other information, covering all of your shares. If your portfolio is substantial, also subscribe to Online REFS.

ix) Get in the habit of always cutting your losses and running your profits.

x) Monitor your investment performance and compare it with the market regularly.

5. Active investment is only worthwhile if it gives you an edge. If you are unable to beat the market by investing directly in shares, you should go back to investing via a tracker fund or through a mechanistic high-yield approach.

11

A TASTE OF TWO METHODS

'Select stocks the way porcupines make love – very carefully.'

Bob Dinda

A key element of becoming a successful active investor is to master a method and to stick with it. There are two main approaches to investment, value and growth, which appeal to different kinds of investor. Although it takes years to become truly expert at active investment, applying the basics of the two methods outlined in this chapter should soon put you on the road to systematic and profitable share selection.

VALUE INVESTING

Value, or contrarian, investing works on a similar principle to the O'Higgins method described in Chapter 9. Rather than focus on dividend yield, however, it uses, among other key investment measures, the price-earnings ratio, to measure the value of a share. The price-earnings ratio is calculated by dividing a company's share price by its earnings per share. These earnings can either be the most recently reported year or alternatively what the earnings analysts expect the company to achieve in the future.

In simple terms, the price-earnings ratio, or PER as it is sometimes known, is a measure of a share's popularity. A high PER indicates that investors are prepared to pay a high price for a company's earnings, usually because they expect them to grow quickly. A low PER, in contrast, is a sign that the market does not rate a company's earnings highly, usually because it expects them to grow slowly if at all.

Contrarian investors buy shares when their PERs are low. The thinking underlying the method is that the market tends to overvalue popular stocks and undervalue unpopular ones. It rests upon extensive research which has proven that buying out-of-favour shares (ie shares with low PERs) can be a highly effective method of beating the market.

As we have seen, there is a strong element of contrarian thinking in the O'Higgins high-yield method. Going against the crowd has been a very effective basis for share selection over long periods of time.

David Dreman

The contrarian approach is closely associated with a very successful American fund manager, David Dreman. His techniques have spawned many imitators in the US, most of whom pay lip-service to the buzzword 'contrarian'. However, few can match his performance. Dreman's Kemper-Dreman High Return Fund has been one of the market leaders since its inception in 1988. He is one of a handful of money managers whose clients have beaten the runaway US market over recent years.

David Dreman's latest book, *Contrarian Investment Strategies: The Next Generation*, explains very clearly the simple logic of his investment approach and demonstrates its impressive track record. The method appears to be a systematic and safe way of buying shares in good companies when they are temporarily out of favour.

His approach is attractive because it provides a safe way of investing in blue-chip stocks, with household names, which make many investors feel more comfortable.

Companies that are consistently generating high rates of earnings growth tend to be highly priced because their large followings are fully aware of their above-average prospects. This can make it difficult to find attractively-priced growth shares among the market's leading shares. Even when the market is high, however, it is always possible to find good investment opportunities among the FTSE 100 shares which for one reason or another have fallen out of favour.

If you are interested in the contrarian method you should first read *Contrarian Investment Strategies: The Next Generation*. It is published by Simon & Schuster in the US but available from leading bookshops and Harriman House, the business bookseller, in the UK (tel: 01730 233 870).

Psychology and stock market investment

At the heart of Dreman's contrarian technique is a fundamental psychological insight: stock market investors over-react. Dreman demonstrates how investors consistently overvalue the so-called 'best' stocks and undervalue the so-called 'worst' stocks. There is a long history of stock market manias from tulip bulbs to internet shares and periods of extreme pessimism about shares, but Dreman's point is that this tendency to overshoot in both directions happens to a lesser degree even in 'normal' markets.

Why current methods don't work

Dreman suggests three major reasons why investors often 'get it wrong':

1. Investors over-emphasise near-term prospects. Because of this they over-price companies when news is good and under-price them when things are not going their way. *Markets are not efficient.*
2. Investors are not realistic. They spend all their time looking for the next Coca-Cola or Microsoft, failing to notice the consistently better value in less fashionable corners of the market. Being natural optimists, *investors are temperamentally unsuited to investing in out-of-favour stocks, even if they understand that the odds are better.*
3. Investors rely too heavily on forecasts of a company's profits and earnings per share. *These have been proven to be unreliable.*

The dangers of forecasting

The most important of these three flaws is the fallibility of forecasts because future expectations are so central in investment. The difficulty of looking into the future was neatly paraphrased by Winston Churchill, who said: 'I prefer not to prophesy before the event. It is much better to prophesy after the event has already taken place.'

If you think about it, the analysts who are employed to forecast the future earnings of companies are placed in an impossible situation. First, they are bombarded with vast amounts of difficult-to-quantify information on such matters as competitive conditions, capacity utilisation rates and pricing. All this varied information must be synthesised and evaluated before the analyst can arrive at an earnings estimate.

On top of the forecasting problems, the analyst must assess management, expansion plans, finances, likely dividends, accounting policies and a host of other complex issues. He or she must also take into account general economic conditions, which means assessing interest rates, unemployment, inflation, industrial production and other economic variables. Economists are often wrong about these things, so the securities analyst is invariably basing assumptions on already flawed data which is changing all the time.

Finally, even if the analyst has made all the correct assumptions and weighed them all up against each other in a rational way, he or she has to overcome the professional pressures that push the City into flattering the prospects of existing or potential clients.

The wonder is not that analysts' forecasts are sometimes wrong, but rather that they are often right.

How surprises affect share prices

Because the market is unable to predict the future accurately, investors are constantly surprised by earnings and other announcements. The key point about these surprises is that they affect share prices in dramatically different and *totally predictable* ways. When a high-flying share fails to match excessive market hopes it is stranded, with no support, and its rapid decline is as inevitable as it is painful. The performance of countless internet and other high-tech stocks during the boom and subsequent bust of 1999 and 2000 provided a graphic recent illustration of this. However, there is a long history of similar gravity-defying runs coming to an abrupt end from radio stocks to the so-called Nifty Fifty back in the 1960s.

In contrast, when a bombed-out share disappoints the market even further than it already has, the impact on its price tends to be minimal. Everyone knows this stock is a disaster, so what difference does one more piece of bad news make?

The flip side of these two tendencies is also apparent. When a high-flying share outperforms expectations, the market tends to shrug its collective shoulders. Everyone knows this is an excellent company – this is the proof. The company finds itself on a treadmill when only the very best is good enough. With a bombed-out stock, when reality turns out to be not so awful as investors had feared, the bounce can be very substantial. Either the market reassesses the share's rating or a predator moves in. Both ways the shareholders win.

Playing safe

Dreman's conclusion is that because most analysts get it wrong most of the time, the most sensible investment approach is to assume the worst. Putting this into practice means avoiding highly-priced shares which depend on high expectations being met. This way you won't be disappointed when over-optimistic forecasts are not achieved.

By concentrating on lowly-priced, out-of-favour shares an investor massively increases his margin of safety. We have already seen one way to recognise out-of-favour shares – a high dividend yield. The simplest other measure is a low price-earnings ratio, although Dreman also proves that buying shares with a low price-to-cashflow and low price-to-book value is also an effective way of beating the market. The November 1998 article from *Investing for Growth* in Appendix II gives a complete picture and also shows you how to get the best from all of these concepts. Read it at leisure after finishing this chapter.

Dreman's track record

Dreman tested his theory in a thorough and very systematic way, using the Standard & Poor's Compustat database of the largest 1,500 companies in the US. He divided these companies into five bands, or quintiles, according to their PER (and separately according to their price-to-cashflow and price-to-book value). The first quintile included the 300 shares with the lowest PERs and so on until the fifth quintile included the 300 shares with the highest PERs.

He then calculated the total return – share price growth plus dividends – for each share within each quintile and produced an average return for each group of shares. This could then be compared with the returns from the other quintiles and with the market as a whole.

Dreman demonstrated that over 27 years there has been a very close correlation on average between the PER (or price-to-cashflow or price-to-book value) of a stock and its subsequent share price outperformance. Shares with a low PER on average outperformed the market between 1970 and 1996 while those with the highest PERs underperformed.

Dreman also showed clearly the *consistency* of the out and underperformance. The group of shares with the lowest PERs achieved an average annual total return of 19 per cent a year between 1970 and 1996. This compared with a total return for the most highly-rated shares of 12.3 per cent and a total return for the market as a whole of 15.3 per cent.

The lowest PER stocks beat the highest by 6.7 per cent a year, which as you already know represents a massive advantage when compounded year after year. To put the difference into context, £1,000 invested at a steady 12.3 per cent a year for 25 years would grow to £18,175. £1,000 invested at a steady 19 per cent would be worth £77,388 after the same length of time.

Consistent outperformance

The trend demonstrated by the Compustat shares when ranked by PER applies just as well when the shares are ranked by price-to-cashflow or by price-to-book value.

In the case of price-to-cashflow, the 300 shares with the lowest ratios generated a total return of 18 per cent a year over the 27 years of the study, while the highest 300 produced only 11.2 per cent. The market as a whole, as we have seen, had a total return of 15.1 per cent. Just as the total returns from the PER quintiles moved progressively lower as the average ratio increased, so the total return decreased as the price-to-cashflow increased. The chart for price-to-book value is almost identical. The 300 share quintile with the lowest price-to-book value had a total return of 18.8 per cent against 12 per cent for the highest quintile. Again, as the price-to-book value increased the total return declined.

An eclectic approach

Obviously, for most investors buying the 300 shares in the market with the lowest PERs is not a realistic proposition, so Dreman suggests using low PER as the first of a series of selection criteria. He describes this combination of a major indicator with a series of ancillary criteria as his 'eclectic approach'. If you choose to adopt a contrarian approach you will also need to develop a combination of criteria which works for you.

Dreman's main ancillary indicators, which help to increase his margin of safety, are:

1. A strong financial position. This helps a company survive periods of trading difficulty.

2. As many favourable operating and financial ratios as possible.

3. A higher rate of earnings growth than the market average and the likelihood that it will not plummet in the near future.

4. Conservative earnings estimates.

5. An above-average dividend yield, which the company can sustain and increase. This is familiar territory for investors who have progressed from the O'Higgins approach.

Finding contrarian investments

So much for the theory. How do you actually go about finding companies which qualify on these selection criteria?

Fortunately, these days it is within the grasp of private investors as much as the professionals to search a database of financial information using criteria such as these. In the last chapter we mentioned REFS, which is the best available tool for finding shares which qualify on a series of statistical measures. It is a simple matter to enter the criteria and print out a list of the shares which meet your criteria.

Without REFS, the work involved in trawling through the accounts of many hundreds of companies would be far too much for an individual investor. For an active investor with serious ambitions there is no alternative to buying REFS or a similar product, if necessary as a shared investment with others or as part of a club.

GROWTH INVESTING

Most active investors tend to be attracted to growth stocks and they are certainly our favourite hunting ground. This is not surprising when you consider some of the fantastic gains that have been achieved by investors lucky enough to catch the best growth shares early. A classic example of this is Coca-Cola, which was floated in 1919 at $40 a share, fell within a year to $20 and by the mid-1990s, with all income reinvested, was worth over $4 million for each original share.

Or take the example of Anne Scheiber who, after retiring from the US Internal Revenue Service, invested $5,000 in the stock market in 1944. When she died in 1995, at the age of 101, her $5,000 had grown to a fortune of $22 million. She invested mainly in leading growth stocks with great business franchises, such as Coca-Cola and Schering-Plough. She did not deal very often, which kept her costs low, and she achieved a compound annual return of 18 per cent, the same as the average total return from the UK market over the past 20 years.

In the UK, we are not so fortunate as investors in the US where there is a much larger number of companies with great business franchises and a much larger domestic market which allows a good business to be rolled out over a much longer period. American cultural imperialism means that really successful brands, such as McDonald's, Disney and Microsoft, are not restricted even to this large home market. The world is their oyster. However, even in the UK the gains from the best-performing growth shares in recent years have been breathtaking.

Take Capita, which has been a huge beneficiary of the ongoing trend towards outsourcing non-core business functions like payroll and shareholder administration. The company collects £1.5bn a year in council tax payments, for example, and issues 12.5 million payslips. Since the end of 1995, its dominance of this white collar outsourcing market has led to a massive rise in its share price from

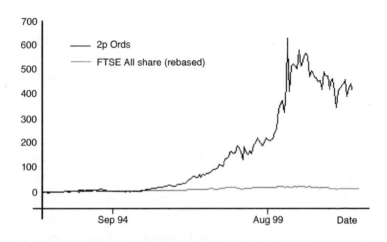

around 30p to today's 426p – an almost 15-fold rise in just over 6 years. During the tech stock boom, as the chart above shows, its shares reached a peak of 645p.

Selection is more important than timing

One reason why growth company investors can gain a material edge is that choosing the right stocks has been proven to be the best way to achieve superior investment returns – much more effective, for example, than timing the market. An interesting study by CDA-Weisenberger tracked the fortunes of two gifted men: Mr A, who had the ability to time the market to perfection and Mr B who had always invested in the best sector. Both investors began with $1,000 on 31 March 1980 and by 30 September 1992, Mr A had been in and out of the market nine times, timing each move to a nicety. His $1,000 had grown to $14,650.

However, Mr B, who had always been fully invested in the best sectors, turned his $1,000 investment into $62,640. During the same period, an investment in the S&P 500 would have grown to a mere $6,030. The results achieved by Mr A and Mr B would, of course, have been almost impossible to emulate, but they do show that *selection is much more important than timing.*

What is a growth share?

The word growth is used to describe shares in companies which have the ability to increase earnings per share (EPS) at an above-average rate year after year. It does not refer to share price growth which is *usually* umbilically linked with earnings growth in the long run but, in the short term, may go up or down for other reasons.

The link, or rather the lack of it, between earnings growth and share price growth was shown graphically during the tech stock boom and bust of 1999 and 2000. In a few mad months, shares in companies which had never made, and were never likely to make, a profit soared as much as ten-fold and more. They subsequently came crashing back down to earth as the long-run linkage between earnings and share prices reasserted itself. As Benjamin Graham put it so well: 'in the short run the market is a voting machine, in the long run it is a weighing machine'.

Real growth stocks tend to share a handful of features. They are usually in 'new economy' sectors such as support services, software or leisure and are unlikely to be in 'old economy' business such as shipbuilding, engineering or textiles. They are also unlikely to be in cyclical sectors such as construction, although in recent years some of the steadiest earnings performers have in fact been housebuilders, once the most cyclical of all stocks!

Most great growth shares enjoy a competitive advantage over their rivals, such as a strong business franchise, patent or brand name. They are very likely to be able to clone their activity and roll it out across the country and hopefully internationally as well.

Finally, great growth stocks will certainly have above-average management. Judging this is very difficult, however, so it is preferable to adopt a more arithmetical approach as the first step in selecting growth shares.

The PEG approach

We encountered the PER with the contrarian value approach. It is certainly the most commonly used investment measure, and you will find it on the prices pages of most newspapers. At the time of writing, even after the fall from grace of the previously high-flying tech stocks, there is still a wide variation in price-earnings ratios, ranging from less than 10 for out-of-favour shares in businesses like housebuilders to more than 40, and sometimes much higher, for flavour-of-the-month stocks in the popular media, IT and support services sector. The tables opposite show a few of the most popular shares together with a selection of the market's most out-of-favour companies in early 2002.

However, the PER is only a one-dimensional measure because it takes no account of the expected growth of a company's earnings per share which is a very important determinant of the appropriate price for a share. For example, a company which has the ability to grow its earnings regularly at 30 per cent a year is obviously worth much more than one which has stagnating earnings or worse.

Far more meaningful is the relationship between a company's PER and its earnings growth rate. We call this measure the price-earnings growth factor, or PEG for short. The PEG is an invaluable investment tool, calculated by

Shooting Stars

Company	PER
BSkyB	92
Egg	72
Carlton Comm.	59
Canary Wharf	47
Autonomy	44
Chrysalis	62
ARM Holdings	55
Capita	40
Schroders	42
GWR Group	39

Out-of-Favour Dogs

Company	PER
Prowting	6
George Wimpey	7
Ashtead	7
British Polythene	7
Clinton Cards	7
Inchcape	8
Brown & Jackson	8
SFI	8
UK Coal	8
Old Mutual	9

dividing a company's PER by its earnings growth rate. Say a company is growing its earnings at 20 per cent a year and its prospective PER is 20, its PEG is 1.0. If it were growing its earnings at a more attractive 30 per cent but it had the same PER, its PEG would be 0.67 and, all other things being equal, it would be a more attractive investment proposition. Broadly speaking, *a share with a low PEG is more attractive than a share with a high PEG*. It provides growth at a reasonable price – GARP for short.

An important aspect of the PEG approach is that it also provides a built-in margin of safety. By selecting shares with a low PER relative to their earnings growth rate, investors minimise the risk that the market will mark down a share price because it is disappointed with the company's results. Even if earnings growth is not quite up to scratch, the shares are unlikely to fall sharply because the rating is already relatively low. By contrast, a high-flying share which disappoints is extremely vulnerable to a painful sell-off.

Even if a share enjoys an attractive PEG factor, it is advisable to avoid shares with high PERs because, in the end, high ratings regress to the norm. This can have a very damaging effect on your long-term performance. Much more attractive is a share with a high growth rate and a relatively low PER. This kind of share is likely to enjoy a wonderful double whammy – its shares will rise in value in line with earnings growth and then rise further still because the market will begin to re-rate the shares of a fast-growing company.

The double whammy

To see how this works in practice, imagine a company which earned 10p per share in its most recent financial year and is forecast to grow its earnings to 12.5p this year, a 25 per cent increase, and 16p next year, a 28 per cent increase. Say the share has a prospective PER of 10, which means its share price is 10 times this year's expected earnings per share – that is 125p.

Now look forward to when the company actually achieves this year's forecast 12.5p earnings per share. At this point the market will begin to anticipate next year's 16p earnings per share. If the PER remains at 10, the shares will rise to 160p, a 28 per cent rise which is in line with the forecast earnings growth. However, in practice a share producing high and accelerating earnings growth in this way could easily attract a higher multiple and the PER would probably rise to at least 15.

By multiplying the forecast earnings per share of 16p by the new higher PER, the share price becomes 240p. Because of the double whammy of earnings growth and a re-rating, the share price has almost doubled. This is why GARP is such an attractive method.

Achieving a margin of safety

Once you have grasped the basic arithmetic of growth stock investing, the next step is to put it into practice in a low-risk way which maximises your chances of picking the stock market's future shooting stars and avoiding its disasters. To do this you must always try to establish an increased margin of safety.

There are nine main ways of doing this:

1. By ensuring there is a past record of earnings growth
2. By assessing the validity of brokers' forecasts
3. By focusing on cash flow
4. By insisting on a strong financial position
5. By looking for accelerating earnings per share
6. By buying shares which are acting well in the market
7. By judging the quality of a company's management
8. By following directors' share dealings
9. By looking for companies with a strong competitive advantage

Let us deal with these in turn.

1. **Past record of earnings growth**

   Before giving a share a PEG, Company REFS requires four years of earnings growth, either historic or a mixture of historic and forecast growth. This means a company can qualify for a PEG if it has already reported two years growth and is forecast to have two more years growth in the future. This is important because, as David Dreman has proved, brokers' forecasts can be unreliable. By insisting on some past earnings growth your assessment is at least grounded in verifiable facts.

2. **Brokers' forecasts**

   Comparing companies on the basis of their estimated future results is, of course, highly dependent on the accuracy of brokers' forecasts. David Dreman's contrarian theory is premised on the fact that analysts often get their estimates wrong. However, investment is largely about future expectations so we recommend taking a few elementary precautions to reduce the risk of being wrong.

   First, check the annual report and interim statement to find out exactly what the chairman has said about future prospects. Also check press cuttings to see if anything has been added at the annual meeting or in interviews with the press. Another useful indicator is the level of dividend paid and/or forecast. If dividends have been steadily rising and are then simply maintained, this can be a sign of trouble ahead.

   Further indicators are more general in nature. For example, the retail sales trends that are announced each month can be a useful pointer to the credibility of a retailer's forecast.

   It is essential to monitor every share in your portfolio

by keeping an eye on the validity of the consensus forecast which, more than anything else, underpins the share price.

3. **Strong cash flow**

   Generalising about investment can be dangerous, but it is invariably the case that shares with excellent cash flow are attractive. The converse is also true – companies which fail to turn their profits into cash are suspect. There is no more reassuring investment than a good growth share with healthy cash balances and strong cash flow per share well in excess of earnings per share. Cash flow is much more difficult to fudge than earnings so an abundance of it provides a measure of protection against creative accounting.

   Many American investors look upon cash flow as the single most important factor in appraising a share. Warren Buffett put it succinctly when he said 'All earnings are not created equal.' He distinguishes between companies that generate surplus cash which can be distributed to shareholders as dividends or spent on genuine expansion and those that need to spend most of their profits on new and replacement plant and machinery *just to stay in business*.

   Healthy cash flow is the life blood of any business and is needed to fund the following:

   - repayment of loans
   - future capital expenditure
   - dividends

A share which has an apparently attractive PEG factor should, therefore, be viewed with suspicion if it cannot also demonstrate strong cash flow.

4. **Strong financial position**

Cash flow per share is only one measure of a company's financial position. The level of gearing, cash balances and general liquidity are also very important indicators of its capacity to survive in difficult times. The most important measure of financial strength is gearing, which shows the company's level of borrowings in relation to the size of the business. It is calculated by taking overall borrowings, subtracting cash or near cash equivalents and expressing the result as a proportion of shareholders' funds. As a general rule, gearing of more than 50 per cent can be a possible cause for concern.

5. **Accelerating earnings per share**

An acceleration in the rate of growth of a company's earnings per share often provides an excellent opportunity for buying its shares cheaply. The reason is simple – it takes a few months for the change in forecast earnings per share, and more importantly, the company's growth rate, to be reflected in the share price.

When a company's growth rate accelerates, its shares benefit from a powerful double whammy. First, the share price rises to reflect its higher than expected earnings per share. Second, the market is very likely to re-rate the shares, putting them on a higher PER to reflect the better prospects. The combination of these two effects can be very substantial.

6. **Relative strength**

The selection criteria used so far narrow the potential universe of growth shares considerably and provide some peace of mind. The next stage is to measure the performance of the shares against that of the market as a whole to see if the company has 'the force' with it. Although it is tempting to think that shares which have underperformed recently have the most potential for growth, in practice the best-performing shares tend to be those which have *already* started acting like winners by outperforming the market.

A few years ago, an American fund manager Jim O'Shaughnessy conducted some research on relative strength using 43 years of data from the Standard & Poor's Compustat database. He tested every conceivable method of investment and found that the 10 best strategies for buying American shares all involved an element of positive relative strength.

Calculating whether relative strength is positive or negative is fairly straightforward. Say the market, as represented by the FT-A All Share index, stands at 1,800 and the share price of a company is 100p. If the market rises by 18 points during the month, it rises by 1 per cent of 1,800. Unless the company's shares rise by at least 1p, their relative strength is negative. If the shares rise by 1p, matching the market's percentage growth, their relative strength is neutral and if the shares rise by more than 1p, their relative strength is positive. Do not worry about how to perform the calculation – services such as Company REFS will do this for you. It is arguable that by insisting on positive relative strength, you will miss the early stages of a share price rise. There is some truth in this, but the margin of safety provided by a share's momentum is very reassuring.

7. **Management**
It is important to ensure, as far as you are able, that the management of any company in which you invest is

both competent and honest. The difficulty arises in judging people from a brief meeting or from reading annual reports, brokers' circulars, magazines and newspapers.

Here are a few guidelines:

- *Annual general meetings.* It is a good idea to attend AGMs to see whether or not they are well organised and how well the chairman and chief executive field questions.
- *Annual reports.* Overly lavish reports, littered with colour photographs, especially of the chairman and directors, are usually a worrying sign.
- *Lifestyle.* Avoid companies with chief executives who live in a flashy way with personalised number plates, aeroplanes and the like. Worry too, if the chief executive is distracted from his core business and buys a stake in a football club.
- *Failure to meet profit forecasts.* This is a very bad sign, which is usually heavily punished by the stock market. Any chief executive who fails to meet a formal profit forecast is on a slippery slope for years to come.

8. **Directors' share dealings**

As a matter of routine you should always check the recent share dealings of a company's directors. The most important point to bear in mind is that buying is far more important than selling. A director investing a significant amount of cash in his or her company presumably feels that the shares are undervalued and are a better investment than cash. The same argument does not always apply in reverse. Directors may sell a share, even if they believe it is fairly priced or undervalued, because they need the cash for any one of several perfectly valid reasons – buying a house being the most frequent.

9. **Competitive advantage**
   The competitive advantage of a company underpins future earnings and increases the reliability of profit forecasts. Sometimes called a 'business franchise', it can arise in several different ways:

   - *Top-class brand names*, such as Coca-Cola and Sony.
   - *Patents or copyrights*, especially these days, when the rapid growth in the internet and digital broadcasting is fuelling an unprecedented demand for high-quality content. Ownership of this content is extremely valuable.
   - *Legal monopolies*, such as broadcasting licences or train operating franchises.
   - *Dominance in an industry*, such as that enjoyed by the *Wall Street Journal* or the *Financial Times*. The internet, far from undermining the positions of existing dominant players like these, could well enhance the value of a brand if people are faced with too wide a choice.
   - *An established position in a niche market*. At the end of 1999, shares in NXT, for example, soared as the market focused on its dominance in the niche of miniaturising loudspeaker technology, a key component of the move towards mobile computing. (Like many others, they subsequently fell sharply in the tech collapse, but when tech stocks come back into favour the market is likely to focus once again on this kind of unassailable technological lead.)

One of the best ways of measuring a company's competitive advantage is the return it achieves on all the capital employed in the business. This ROCE is calculated by expressing pre-tax profit before all borrowing costs as a percentage of the capital employed in the company.

The second key indicator of a strong competitive advantage is the kind of margin that a company can obtain on its products or services. Margin is the ratio of operating profit to turnover. The profit margin of a company should be compared with the margins of other companies in its peer group and with the sector average. The trend is crucial because falling margins can be the first warning signal that a company is losing its competitive advantage.

Other investment criteria

As well as a low PEG and the margin of safety features already listed, a growth stock investor needs to consider several other criteria:

1. **Low market capitalisation**
   In certain phases of the market, large companies outperform smaller companies and vice versa. In 1999, for example, smaller companies massively out-performed blue-chip shares but this performance came after several years of significant underperformance. Active investors can focus on either large or small companies and their approach will largely be determined by their temperament.

   While it is obviously true that a company capitalised at £10 million will find it much easier to double in size than one worth £1 billion, there are drawbacks to investing in very small companies. Share prices can come under pressure if market makers find themselves with too much stock or the market's mood turns bearish. Also the spread between the buying and selling price of a smaller stock can be relatively large and, in some cases, it can be difficult dealing in a sufficient quantity in an illiquid stock.

However, the main advantage of investing in smaller companies is that they tend to be less well-researched than larger businesses. This means you are more likely to benefit from the eventual upward correction of a serious pricing anomaly.

2. **Dividend yield**

In itself, a substantial dividend yield is of no real importance to a growth investor. Warren Buffett always argues that retained earnings are of more use to shareholders as growth companies use the money for expansion and can make an excellent return on the capital. However, an attractive dividend yield helps to support a share price. Most investors prefer growth stocks to pay dividends, even if they are small and there are some funds which will only invest in companies if they pay a dividend.

3. **Companies buying in their own shares**

It is usually a very bullish sign when a company announces that it intends to buy in its own shares. First, it shows the confidence of the board in the company and it usually implies that the company's liquidity is strong. Second, the supply of the company's shares is tightened as shares overhanging the market are mopped up. Third, buying in shares is usually earnings-enhancing.

4. **Something new**

This can often be a good reason to buy a company's shares. The something in question usually falls into one of four categories:

- new management
- new technology or new products
- new events in the industry as a whole, including new legislation
- new acquisitions.

5. **Low price-to-sales ratio**

Jim O'Shaughnessy's research has shown that a low price-to-sales ratio (PSR), coupled with high relative strength over the previous 12 months, is one of the most potent combinations of investment criteria. The PSR is mainly used to spot recovery situations. It is also particularly useful when a company begins to make losses and, as a result, has no PER with which to value the shares.

Finding out more about growth shares

If you are attracted by the prospect of investing directly in growth shares and trying your hand at finding the next Coca-Cola or Sage, you should read *The Zulu Principle* and then *Beyond The Zulu Principle* by Jim Slater. This will take you through the whole process of growth stock investing from first principles.

It shows why you should invest in growth shares, how the PEG works and how it can be further enhanced by choosing stocks with strong cash flow and good relative strength against the market. It also explains competitive advantage and shows you how to pinpoint good management and how to measure a company's financial position. Finally, there are chapters on how to manage your portfolio of growth stocks through bull and bear markets and an extensive list of further recommended reading.

Growth stock investing in practice

To illustrate the lure and excitement of active investment in growth stocks, here is an outstandingly successful example of a recommendation from the Hemscott Analyst email share tips service. It shows clearly why anyone with serious financial ambitions is unlikely to settle for the relatively pedestrian performance of a tracker fund or be satisfied with the passive approach of the high-yield method.

Ottakar's

Hemscott Analyst first recommended this bookshop chain in December 2000 when its shares were 55p. At the time, they were still in the doldrums after a catastrophic profit warning shortly after the company floated sent the stock into freefall.

At the time of the recommendation, however, trading was picking up and the shares appeared to be trading on a ludicrously low rating when compared with the expected growth rate. The prospective price-earnings ratio of 6 compared with forecast earnings growth of 52 per cent.

By April 2002, the shares had soared on the back of a series of encouraging trading statements to 186p, more than three times the recommendation price in just 18 months. Even after the rise, the shares traded on a prospective price-earnings ratio of only 11, with earnings of 25 per cent forecast for the following 12 months.

This example demonstrates the kind of gain that can be achieved by investing in a well-chosen growth stock. Of course, many growth stocks perform in a much more pedestrian way and a few fail completely. That is why it is so important to get into the habit of cutting losses and running profits.

Active growth stock investment will not suit every investor's temperament but for any with serious financial ambitions it is a key ingredient in their bid to become a millionaire and achieve financial freedom. Finding a few winners like Ottakar's is also great fun. It is this kind of success that makes investment 'the best game in town'.

SUMMARY

1. There are two main approaches to active investment – value and growth.
2. Value investing focuses on out-of-favour shares with low PERs, low prices-to-cashflow or low prices-to-book value.
3. American investor David Dreman has demonstrated that over extended periods lowly-rated shares have outperformed their highly-rated peers.
4. If you want to learn more about value investing, read *Contrarian Investment Strategies: The Next Generation* by David Dreman (Simon & Schuster).
5. Most active investors focus on growth shares, which have produced the stock market's most exciting gains.
6. Growth stock investing focuses on the relationship between a share's PER and its expected earnings growth rate – the PEG factor.
7. As well as a low PEG, growth stock investors should

look for strong cashflow and high relative strength against the market.

8. In addition to these main selection criteria, growth stock investors should concentrate on:

    - a satisfactory past record of earnings growth
    - the validity of brokers' forecasts
    - a company's management
    - directors' dealings
    - a company's competitive advantage
    - a company's financial position
    - whether earnings growth is accelerating.

9. Other important factors to consider include:

    - market capitalisation
    - dividend yield
    - price-to-sales ratio
    - if a company is buying in its own shares
    - something new.

10. If you are interested in learning more about growth stock investing, read *The Zulu Principle* and *Beyond The Zulu Principle* by Jim Slater.

12

TEN STEPS TO FINANCIAL FREEDOM

'The future will be better tomorrow.'

Dan Quayle

You do not need to win the Lottery to become a millionaire. It can be a much more certain process and, as Chairman Mao was fond of saying – a long march begins with a single step.

Here are the ten steps which will launch you on your bid to become a millionaire and secure your financial freedom.

1. **Harness the power of compounding**
   Understand and harness the power of compounding as early as possible in your life. Compounding is the eighth wonder of the world and you must put it to work for you and your family at the earliest opportunity.

   Remember too that inflation is always working insidiously against you – a hidden tax that is constantly diminishing your wealth. Your aim is, of course, to beat inflation by a wide margin and that is why your basic plan should be to put two prime financial assets to work against it on your behalf.

2. **Buy your own home**
   Buy your own house or flat at the earliest opportunity, a wonderful way of increasing your capital, completely tax-free, that has already enriched millions of UK citizens.

Remember the most important rule when buying property – position is more important than condition. You are better off buying the worst house in the best road than the best house in the worst road.

3. **Avoid endowment policies**

When financing your home, avoid endowment mortgages. If you already have one, check the surrender value and, using the tables in Chapters 4 and 5, calculate if it makes sense to surrender. Remember that you will usually be able to improve upon the insurance company's offer by auction or through a specialist broker in the market. It invariably pays to surrender endowment policies if they are in their early or mid-way stages. It is more doubtful when a policy is nearing maturity.

If you are in any doubt whatsoever about surrendering you should obtain independent financial advice. The key word here is 'independent'. As you know, endowment policies have structured within them hefty commissions for the firms that make the sales so it is vital to make sure that the adviser is not remunerated by commission on the products you are discussing.

4. **Obtain an ISA mortgage**

Finance the purchase of your home with an ISA mortgage. The beauty of this approach is that you will be able to harness the power of compounding much more effectively by putting two top-class financial assets to work for you at the same time and, most importantly, both will be *free of tax*. With an ISA you can accumulate capital in shares which on all measures of past performance should increase in value at a much greater rate than the cost of the extra interest on the

part of the mortgage that you would have otherwise
repaid.

At present, any capital gain on your house is tax-free.
Moreover, any capital gain on shares held in an ISA is
tax-free and so is the income from the shares. These
two privileges massively enhance future capital gains
and you should, therefore, make the maximum possible
use of them. In particular, try to take up your annual
ISA allowance each year both for yourself and your
spouse. Also, when planning how to minimise your
annual capital gains tax, remember to take full
advantage of the annual capital gains tax allowance for
yourself and your spouse.

5. **Invest with a regular savings plan**
   Make sure that you invest *regularly* with a savings plan
   to avoid being caught by a sudden downturn in the
   market. Over the last 85 years, shares have always
   beaten cash or gilts in every three-year period. This
   holds good for periods that include the horror years for
   the market – 1929, 1974 and 1987. The key point is to
   keep investing regularly, however bleak the outlook
   appears to be at the time. By *averaging* in this way,
   some of your investments will be at lower levels and
   make up for the losses on the instalments at higher
   levels. Eventually, the overall upward trend of the
   market should yield you a very satisfactory return. A
   regular savings plan can be set up through a unit trust
   if you are investing in tracker funds, or through a
   broker if you are selecting your own shares.

6. **Invest in tracker funds**
   You can eliminate the risk of investing in the wrong
   stocks year after year by investing in a pooled fund

which simply strives to keep pace with the market averages. This can be done easily by using FT-A All Share tracker funds managed by a well-known group such as Gartmore, Legal & General, M&G, Norwich Union or Virgin and setting up a regular savings plan with them.

7. **Or, use a mechanical system to select your own shares**
   A more ambitious alternative to a tracker is to set up an ISA of your own through a stockbroker and to use the high-yield selection system explained in Chapter 9. This proven method, which will take you less than one hour a year to put into practice, has beaten the market by a comfortable margin over many years.

8. **Or, become an active investor**
   If you want to explore the stock market further and become more proficient at value or growth stock investment, it is essential to read some of the excellent books on the subject before you begin your journey. You should also join an investment club through ProShare (tel: 020 7220 1750) to benefit from interaction with other investors.

   It is also vital to obtain a reliable source of statistical and clear information, covering all your shares. If your portfolio is substantial enough, it would pay to subscribe to CD REFS or Online REFS.

   Great growth shares are the best possible investments but it is obviously essential to choose the right ones and it is hard to be right even 70 per cent of the time. That is why it is important to cut losses and run profits. You will get out of investment what you put into it, so if you are interested now is the time to get started.

9. **Monitor your performance**

Whichever kind of investor you become, it is vitally important to monitor your performance against the market. Even with tracker funds, make sure that the disparity between your fund's performance and the market's is tolerable compared with other similar funds. With the high-yield system, carefully measure your performance against the market, including the average dividend yield.

If you progress to growth or contrarian value stocks, it is even more important to measure your success. If after a couple of years you find that you are slipping well behind the market, switch back to a tracker fund or the high-yield method and give your personal attention to a more productive area for you.

10. **Keep learning and enjoying the game**

We hope you benefit from this blueprint for financial freedom and progress through all the steps to become a successful active investor. To achieve this, you will need to carry on learning about investment, which we believe is the best game in town. It is tremendous fun, very enriching and can be carried on at almost any age in the comfort of your own home.

We feel that it is vitally important for young people to understand the power of compounding and the broad thrust of this book. Please pass your copy on to the younger members of your family, or better still buy them a copy. If it only helps them to understand the power of compounding and the necessity of beginning to invest early in life, you will have helped to set them on the road to financial freedom. There are few greater gifts.

APPENDIX I

The methodology used for testing the O'Higgins method in the UK:

The test of the O'Higgins method in the UK combines data from an earlier study conducted by Johnson Fry in 1994 with new data procured specifically for this analysis. The results for the first 10 years of the test period (the Johnson Fry study) are taken directly from *Pep Up Your Wealth* by Jim Slater (Orion, 1994). The results for the final five years were compiled and combined with the earlier data by Tom Stevenson in October 1999.

In both cases, a UK portfolio of five stocks was selected by applying the criteria used by O'Higgins in America. First, the 10 highest-yielders were taken from the 30 companies with the largest market capitalisations in the FTSE 100. The lists of the 30 companies used in the 1994–1998 test were supplied by the Stock Exchange from its annual Fact File. From the lists of the 10 highest-yielders, the five shares with the lowest prices, the second lowest-priced share and the second highest-yielding share were selected.

The strategy shadowed by the test was to simply buy the chosen portfolio or single share and hold it for one year, at the end of which the stock or stocks were sold. All proceeds from the sale of the shares *together with the gross dividends received* during the year were then used to purchase new shares, which were again selected using the O'Higgins method. This process was repeated on each anniversary date, which was as close to the last trading day of each calendar year as possible.

In all the calculations, it was assumed that *gross* dividends were not reinvested when paid but at the end of the year during which the selected stocks were held. It was also assumed that no interest was earned on dividend cash payments while awaiting reinvestment and that ACT was reclaimed in time for reinvestment at the end of the year. Although ACT has now been abolished, it was relevant in all 15 years of the test.

Performance comparisons of portfolios constructed using the O'Higgins method were all made using total returns. The definition of the annual total return of any portfolio, with dividends reinvested annually, was the sum of the capital return, which was the price gain or loss, plus all dividend payments and tax reclaimed. This total cash gain for the year was then expressed as a percentage of the original purchase price of the portfolio to provide the total return.

All calculations between 1984 and 1994 were based on data supplied by Datastream, now part of Primark. Stock prices and dividend yields were adjusted for capital reorganisations to calculate price gains and losses and to identify the shares with the highest yield. Historic unadjusted prices were used to select the lowest-priced shares. All calculations from 1995 to 1998 used data taken from Hemmington Scott's (now HS Financial Publishing's) Company REFS. The same adjustments for capital changes were made as in the first 11 years.

To calculate the actual cash dividends paid in any of the first 11 years of the test, it was necessary to work back from Datastream's dividend yield history and the share prices at the *end* of each year to determine the cash payout during the preceding year. By expressing this as a percentage of the share price at the start of the relevant year the dividend component of the total return could be calculated. For the Hemmington Scott years, it was simply assumed that the cash dividend implied by the *forecast* yield used in Company REFS was actually paid during the subsequent 12 months. This figure was then added to the capital gain to calculate the total return.

If a stock was acquired or merged into another, it was sold at the date of change and the total return to that point was used as the total return for the entire year. Datastream's total return index for the All Share index was used for all performance comparisons in all 15 years. This index was based upon adjusted prices and yields and assumed that gross dividends were reinvested when paid.

APPENDIX II

The following text is extracted from an article which was written by Tom Stevenson and Jim Slater in the November 1998 issue of *Investing for Growth*.

Many investors are attracted by the potential for high capital gains from smaller growth shares but are put off by their perceived risk and volatility. Starting this month, we will offer them a constructive alternative by showing how to find some 'safety-first' blue-chip investments to complement our core growth stock recommendations. Subscribers can then balance their portfolios to suit their personal risk profile and income requirements. We have been worried recently that we have been unable to recommend blue-chip shares in *Investing for Growth*. As most subscribers will be aware, we feel that there is very little value in leading stocks in the top quartile of the FTSE 100 index. For example, Glaxo Wellcome, with its heavy weighting of 6 per cent of the index, is on a prospective price-earnings ratio (PER) of 34, with forecast growth of only 13 per cent.

Although these kinds of share seem to us to be absurdly priced, they may move higher still. We believe, however, that there is massive scope for their prices to fall substantially in due course, especially if the companies disappoint the market even to the slightest degree. On a risk/reward ratio basis the shares are, therefore, a poor bet.

We have consistently advised that the best value is

obtainable in SmallCap stocks, many of which can now be bought on below average PERs, well below their prospective growth rates. In the long term, their outstanding value should be recognised and the shares in question should rise substantially – not only in proportion to their earnings growth, but also from the upward status change in their PERs.

The greater value available among smaller companies is good news for active investors who feel comfortable at this end of the market. We are the first to acknowledge, however, that not all investors are happy to weight their portfolios so heavily in SmallCap stocks. Many private investors are reassured by the solidity and permanence of large cap companies. Others may need a higher income and for most institutions the greater liquidity in leading shares is a necessity.

The good news for more conservative investors is that we have just finished reading a remarkable book, which has transformed our thinking about the top end of the market. From this issue onwards, we will be able to recommend a few blue-chip shares with confidence. They will be shares which we believe should have a substantial chance of beating the market without undue risk.

A remarkable book

The book that grabbed our minds was *Contrarian Investment Strategies: The Next Generation*, by David Dreman. The sub-heading, *Beat the Market by Going Against the Crowd*, illustrates its theme.

David Dreman manages the Kemper-Dreman High Return fund in the US, which has been a leader since its inception in 1988 – the number one equity-income fund of all the 208 ranked by Lipper Analytical Services.

Dreman proves by very detailed research covering almost 200 years that shares have been by far the best medium of investment, always substantially beating bonds and cash over any long period. He turns conventional wisdom on its head by proving conclusively that *stocks are by far the least risky investment over time.*

During the 30 years ended 1996, for example, he shows that US shares would have produced a compound return *after inflation* of 780 per cent, compared with only 29.4 per cent for bonds and 13.5 per cent for cash in T-bills.

The performance of shares in Dreman's studies was based on the average medium to large company. However, he goes on to show ways in which returns can be dramatically improved by understanding how much investors overreact to both good news and bad. He argues that glamour stocks can become ridiculously over-priced while out-of-favour shares become outstanding bargains in relation to their underlying value. The key to investment success is to take advantage of this breakdown in the so-called 'efficient market'.

Dreman points out that glamour stocks and out-of-favour, more pedestrian shares, let's call them stalwarts, react to unexpected news in diametrically opposite ways. High-flyers cannot stand bad news, however slight, whereas stalwarts have much greater tolerance and far more resistance to it.

Good news is often in the price of glamour stocks – they are expected to beat their forecasts, often by substantial margins, whereas good news for stalwarts can cause a relatively substantial change in the fundamentals and a massive change in the market's perception of the shares.

Dreman believes these reactions are important because earnings surprises are so common. He explains that brokers' consensus forecasts cannot be relied upon. Having analysed over 94,000 consensus forecasts based on at least four analysts' estimates, covering the period 1973–1996, Dreman found the average annual error rate was 44 per cent. Even eliminating very small companies, the annual error rate was still 23 per cent. Dreman argues that using a contrarian investment approach to focus on the out-of-favour stalwarts and shun over-hyped glamour stocks will allow you to benefit from these forecasting errors.*

Finding the contrarian gems

Contrarian stocks can be found using several criteria, four of which Dreman analyses in great detail. His favourite is a low historic PER, followed closely by low price-to-cash flow, then low price-to-book value and lastly a high dividend yield. He analyses the results from each method during the 27 years from 1970 to 1996 by dividing the whole universe of the largest 1500 US companies on the Compustat database into quintiles (equal fifths). He demonstrates that the quintile with the lowest PER, for example, showed an average annual overall return of 19 per cent, the second lowest quintile showed 17.4 per cent, the middle quintile 14.6 per cent and the last two quintiles with the highest PERs 13.1 per cent and 12.3 per cent. The market performance was roughly in line with the middle quintile, with a return of 15.3 per cent. As you can readily see from the bar chart overleaf, the results are consistent and demonstrate clearly that the lower the PER, the better the overall return in relation to the market.

* Note to growth stock investors – *We do not share Dreman's extreme scepticism about brokers' consensus forecasts. Each broker's forecast needs to be examined carefully, the standard deviation considered and the consensus weighted towards the most recent forecasts. We much prefer to be armed with a well-prepared brokers' consensus forecast rather than the alternative of having no estimates to go on. Although there are sometimes downward revisions, surprises can also happen on the upside.*

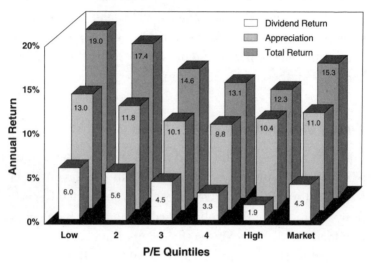

Price/Earnings
Dividends, Appreciation & Total Returns
January 1, 1970 – December 31, 1996

Source: *Contrarian Investment Strategies*

Dreman also analyses price-to-cash flow returns and
price-to-book value returns in a similar way. The lowest
quintile for price-to-cash flow showed an average overall
return of 18 per cent compared with 18.8 per cent for price-
to-book value (and the 19 per cent for low PERs mentioned
earlier). However, the most remarkable feature of Dreman's
study was that exactly the same pattern was produced by
all three studies – the lowest quintiles worked best,
followed by the second lowest. The middle quintiles were,
as might be expected, broadly in line with the market and
the remaining two quintiles, with the highest price-to-cash
flows and price-to-book values, produced returns below the
market average. The charts at the top of these pages
highlight how remarkably similar the patterns are using
PERs and price-to-cash flow.

The high yielders showed a broadly similar pattern but

Price/Cash Flow
Dividends, Appreciation & Total Returns
January 1, 1970 – December 31, 1996

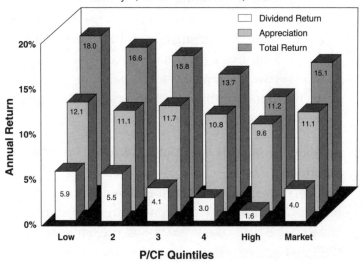

Source: *Contrarian Investment Strategies*

were not quite so convincing. The highest-yielding quintile showed 16.1 per cent, the second highest 17.5 per cent, the middle quintile was about the same as the market and the two quintiles with the lowest yields performed worst.

Ratcheting up returns

Dreman's thesis gets really interesting when he turns his attention to ways of further improving returns. He suggests 'an eclectic approach' which combines several of his methods. For example, assuming you were using the lowest PER as your basic criterion, you could also insist on the shares in question having a low price-to-cash flow (PCF) and a relatively high dividend yield. We very much favour this approach, which seems to us to harness three of the best horses to work as a team.

Dreman recommends using five other eclectic criteria:

1. **A strong financial position.**
   This has always been one of our key measures. The low
   PCF provides some reassurance in this respect but it is
   also crucial to make sure that the company does not
   have excessive borrowings, to measure current assets
   against current liabilities and to ensure that interest
   cover is satisfactory.

2. **As many favourable operating and financial ratios as
   possible.**
   The only criteria that Dreman mentions specifically in
   his case studies are return on equity and improving
   margins. We also like to see a low price-to-sales ratio
   (PSR), which we believe is a better value measure than
   a low price-to-book value (PBV).

3. **A higher rate of earnings growth than the market
   average in the immediate past, and the likelihood that
   it will not plummet in the near future.**
   You will notice that Dreman's approach is beginning to
   share many characteristics with our method of investing
   in SmallCap shares with low PEGs. In spite of Dreman's
   scepticism about brokers' consensus forecasts, he
   prefers to see them rather than fly blind. He explains
   that he only looks for the general direction in the
   forecasts, not the precise figures. In terms of priorities,
   he seems to be far more insistent on ensuring that the
   company's earnings are not about to drop off a cliff
   rather than worrying about a patchy past growth rate.

4. **Earnings estimates should always lean to the
   conservative side.**
   Dreman mentions here the magic words 'margin of

safety' and recommends being very conservative. One obvious interpretation of this is to use the lowest forecast from a reputable broker even if it is well below the consensus. Another is to apply a small percentage reserve for contingencies against the consensus forecast.

5. **An above average yield, which the company can sustain and increase.**
   A high dividend yield makes great sense, especially in a bearish climate and many investors need a good income from their portfolios. Last month, we wrote about O'Higgins's approach to the Dogs of the Dow. This method has worked well in the US during most of the past two decades but we much prefer Dreman's idea of coupling an attractive yield with a low PER and PCF.

A good question at this point is 'When do you sell?' The answer is very simple – as soon as the key measures by which you bought move above the average instead of being well below it. For example, if you purchased a share on a historic PER of 12, below the market average at the time of say 18, you would sell it when the PER rises above the *current* market average. Dreman rightly recommends dealing as infrequently as possible as, otherwise, transaction costs become very expensive and affect relative performance. He also makes it very clear that it is vitally important to take a long-term view and be patient. The odds are firmly on your side, but you have to allow sufficient time for them to work their way through.

Common features

Although apparently unalike, our approach and Dreman's have more common features than differences. Dreman has a lot of time for the GARP approach (growth at a reasonable price), which we use extensively. He is particularly impressed when it is used in conjunction with low PERs. Looking at our recommendations in the core portfolio, it is very clear to us that the recommendations with low PERs have performed better as a group than those with high PERs. The lower PERs provide more resistance to sharp falls and also provide more upside potential if earnings are better than expected. As Dreman says, 'a good GARP situation allows you the possibility of a home run while sitting firmly in the value camp'.

With large cap companies, we have been unable to find GARP situations. However, Dreman's exhaustive research and analysis makes it clear where relative value lies and the safest way of outperforming the market in the large cap arena.

Even with large caps, there is still a great deal in common between our approaches. We favour low PERs, low PCFs, above average growth rates, good relative strength, and an attractive ROE coupled with rising margins. However, the main thrust of our approach is to find shares on low PERs in relation to their prospective growth rates and with other attractive criteria (such as strong cash flow per share in excess of EPS) to make sure that all other things are reasonably equal.

Dreman's approach centres on low PERs, low PCFs, low PBVs and high yields, preferably working in conjunction with each other and also satisfying other criteria such as low gearing and a reasonable return on equity.

His basic idea is that any shares with low PERs, low PCFs, low PBVs and high yields have become unpopular and neglected due to investors overreacting to bad or disappointing news. As a result, the shares often fall to absurdly low levels in relation to the companies' records, positions in their industries and future prospects.

As soon as corporate news improves, Dreman hopes for some growth in EPS and, much more importantly, for a major re-rating of the PER. Dreman's research and the soundness of his method give us great confidence in recommending leading shares that measure up (or should we say down?) to his demanding criteria.

We are grateful to David Dreman for opening up another important investment window for us. We are very hopeful that, as a result, we will be able to help subscribers to invest in leading shares over the long term.

INDEX

ABOUT TEXERE

TEXERE seeks to become the most progressive and authoritative voice in business publishing by cultivating and enhancing ideas that will illuminate the global business landscape. Our name defines the spirit of our vision: TEXERE is the ancient Latin verb "to weave". In an increasingly global business community, we seek to create an intersection where authors and readers can share the best thinking and the latest ideas. We want to leverage the expertise and insights of leading thinkers by weaving them with TEXERE's capability to deliver them to the marketplace. To learn more and become a part of our community visit us at:

www.etexere.com

and

www.etexere.co.uk

ABOUT THE TYPEFACE

This book was set in 10.5/15pt Melior. The Melior typeface was designed by Hermann Zapf, a contemporary German calligrapher, and was released by the Stempel foundry in 1952. It has a straightforward but elegant design that is ideal for business applications.

ABOUT THE AUTHORS

Jim Slater is a Chartered Accountant who for the ten years from 1964 to 1974 was Chairman of the legendary financial conglomerate, Slater Walker Securities. He is generally recognised as an authority on stock markets with an uncanny ability to identify under-valued companies and read market trends.

More recently, Jim Slater has devised Really Essential Financial Statistics (REFS) in conjunction with Hemmington Scott. REFS is a monthly investment service which is popular with private investors and institutions alike.

Jim Slater's previous books, *The Zulu Principle*, *Beyond the Zulu Principle* and *Investment Made Easy* have all been bestsellers.

Tom Stevenson has been a leading financial journalist for 13 years. He was City Editor of *The Independent* and is currently Head of Research and website editor at financial information group Hemscott. He lives in Gloucestershire.